The Internet made easy
by the world's No.1

AOL

Shopping
and Travel

The Internet made easy by the world's No.1

Shopping
and Travel

Safe and easy booking, buying and bargains online

By Steve Shipside

CAPSTONE

Copyright © AOL (UK) Ltd 2002

The right of AOL UK to be identified as the author of this work has been asserted
in accordance with the Copyright, Designs and Patents Act 1988

First published 2002 by
Capstone Publishing Limited (a Wiley company)
8 Newtec Place
Magdalen Road
Oxford OX4 1RE
United Kingdom
http://www.capstoneideas.com

All rights reserved. Except for the quotation of short passages for the purposes of
criticism and review, no part of this publication may be reproduced, stored in a
retrieval system, or transmitted, in any form or by any means, electronic, mechani-
cal, photocopying, recording or otherwise, without the prior permission of the
publisher.

CIP catalogue records for this book are available from the British Library
and the US Library of Congress

ISBN 1-84112-178-9

Typeset in 9.5/14pt Fruitiger by
Sparks Computer Solutions Ltd, Oxford, UK
http://www.sparks.co.uk
Printed and bound by
T.J. International Ltd, Padstow, Cornwall

This book is printed on acid-free paper

Substantial discounts on bulk quantities of Capstone books are available to
corporations, professional associations and other organizations. Please contact
John Wiley & Sons for more details on 212 850 6000 or (fax) 212 850 6088 or
(email) info@wiley-capstone.co.uk

Contents

Shopping Till You (Virtually) Drop

Ask the passengers next to you on a plane what they paid for the flight and you'll be hard pushed to find two people who've paid the same amount.* Full fares, Apex, discount deals, charters, block bookings; they all contribute to a complete pick 'n' mix of prices even within economy class. Trying to find the best deal in all of that once meant having access either to extensive insider knowledge, the luxury of advanced bookings, total flexibility, or a relative in the airline. Now, however, all you need is access to the Web. One of the great promises of shopping on the Web is that it offers so much instant information about products and services, complete with price comparisons, and all without the inconvenience of salespeople, or the overhead fees of shops. Whatever it is you want to buy, from shoes to submarines, the Web can help you find the best deal wherever in the world it happens to be, then serve it directly to your doorstep (for a modest delivery charge, naturally).

With online shopping there is no legwork, no aching feet, and no parking tickets.

---

*If anyone ever does turn to you and ask how much you paid for the flight take my advice; tell them it cost £37.60, all tax included, and watch them wriggle in their seat all the way to your final destination.

Fig. I.1 Type the word and up pop more ideas than you can shake a credit card at.

So why should you shop online at all? Well, for all the scare stories (and a lot of them are no more than stories) the promise of the Web still holds true when it comes to a great many purchases. It's just a question of understanding what it does well, and the steps you can take to ensure you get exactly what you want. Read on and you'll find out exactly how and why you should cyber shop, where to unearth the best deals, and above all, how to ensure that cyber space is a safe place to shop.

1 Saving money

The main reason most people go online to shop in the first place is to save money. Because a virtual shop has no floor space to rent and often fewer staff to pay, it can sometimes afford to discount quite heavily compared to its high street rivals. In some cases the Web provides a way of buying directly from the supplier without the need for a middle man and that can lead to considerable savings. It also provides a way of buying goods from other countries, particularly the States, where some things such as CDs are much cheaper. There are even auctions with the prospect of a fabulous deal at a low price, as well as sites where you can say what you're prepared to pay, and wait for suppliers around the world to decide if they want to take it or leave it. Plus the Web offers a unique example of people power with sites such as LetsBuyIt.com which allow complete strangers to get together, agree on an item they all want to buy, and then use their sheer numbers to demand (and get) bulk discounts from the manufacturers. A look at LetsBuyIt.com's prices over the last year show that on items like Sony TVs the average saving on list price was £400.

No doubt about it, there are great bargains to be had on the Web, and if you've got online access there's no reason why you shouldn't benefit from them. Just a word of warning, however. Not all bargains are what they seem, and more than one happy shopper has made a saving by buying from another country only to have their goods arrive accompanied by a VAT bill from Customs and Excise.

If you want to know just how to look a gift horse in the mouth (remember the Trojans), turn to **Chapter 2, Windows Shopping**.

2 Windows Shopping

2 Saving time

Difficult though it is to believe, there may come a time when you tire of the myriad delights of the supermarket. One day you may find yourself dreaming of an existence free of wonky trolleys, checkout queues, backbreaking carrier bags, and other people's children. Not to mention the small fact that you may want to shop outside of normal shopping hours, or on bank holidays, or indeed at any time you choose, any day of the year. At which point you may want to take a closer look at the online shopping on offer from supermarkets. When you've taken into account the delivery charge, you're unlikely to ever save money by having your groceries delivered, but if you're short of time or the chauffeur's taken the afternoon off you'll be glad to know you can have your spuds delivered to your door or desk.

Alternatively, it could just be that you don't know what to get for that certain someone and realise that looking for inspiration could cost you a day at least in the high streets. Here the Web really excels since entire cyber streets of shops are merely seconds away, some of which are smart enough to act as personal shoppers. Just tell them who the gift is for and what you want to spend and they'll come up with all that thoughtfulness for you.

Whether you're strapped for time, stuck for transport, or short on ideas, then the Web is the answer for you.

3 Saving your bacon

Not only can the Web deliver bacon to your door, it can also do its best to save yours. Why rely on yourself to remember those crucial birthdays and an-niversaries when your computer can not only do it for you but offer to send flowers/gift vouchers right there and then? Knowing your way around online could mean the difference between being able to go back home safely to your family and loved ones, or looking forward to a night in the dog house (also available online if need be).

4 Exotica

Remember there's a whole world in 'www' and that means a planetful of choice. Books that are long out of print in this country can often be found on the other side of the Atlantic. The latest in T-shirts from Tokyo, the most obscure Welsh cheese, you name it. If your taste is at all unusual by the stand-ards of your high street you can be sure that you'll find specialist shops that cater for it online. Just remember to read the notes in **Chapter 2, Windows Shopping** to make sure that your cut-price import doesn't wing its way to you with some equally exotic extra charges or limitations attached.

2 Windows Shopping

5 Because you can get something for nothing.

For some products it is possible to download free samples directly from the Web. Software and games are often available in cut-down trial versions online and can often be upgraded 'instantly' (check on download times in **Chapter 2, Windows Shopping**) to the full version without ever leaving the house or office. Music too is widely available as samples to try before you buy, whether your taste runs to Beethoven or Belgian Techno. Increasingly, the same looks set to be true of video, particularly as bandwidth (the speed at which information can be delivered) increases. In many cases this kind of 'try before you buy' service is simply not available any other way.

2 Windows Shopping

Fig. I.2   AOL will help even the Net newbie to find the online bargains.

6 Because there's no other way at all

For some products and services the Web isn't just the cheapest way of ordering, it's the only way. Where margins are at a premium the Web can be the key to a manufacturer's success or survival, and some simply may not be able to afford more conventional channels. Cut-price airline, easyJet, estimates that in order to fill a plane on a short haul trip the cost of mounting the telesales operation adds up to nearly twice the price of the fuel. Online booking can halve that cost, so where price is the key selling point there is a big incentive for companies to move towards Web-only selling.

All of which make online a compelling place for a spot of retail therapy, or would do if it weren't for those entirely understandable fears about just how safe it is. So let's take a look at just what the risks are, and what can be done to make cyberspace a safe place to spend.

Safe Shopping

According to the Consumer Association's annual survey of Internet users, more than half of UK surfers agree that shopping online is cheaper than buying in the high street. The year before only a quarter of Net users felt that to be true, so the bargain hunter's message seems to be spreading nicely. Except that the same survey showed that over half of UK surfers also felt that it is simply not safe to use a credit card online – a feeling that has only increased since the previous year's survey. That has to be the ultimate consumer frustration: we can see the same goods for less, but we're afraid that if we flash our flexible friends we'll leave ourselves open to fraud.

It's a feat that seems pretty firmly backed up by the headlines. In March 2000 FBI agents descended on the tiny Welsh village of Clynderwen to seize a 19-year-old hacker as part of an investigation into an alleged $3million worth of credit card fraud. The hacker was duly hauled off and accused of hacking Web sites to obtain credit card numbers, including that of billionaire Bill Gates. Reports that the teenager had only used the card number to order the Microsoft boss a delivery of Viagra may have raised a few smiles, but the story didn't do anything to reassure the Web-wary consumer. Which is a shame, because for all the splash that hacker stories make, the dangers of cyber shopping are greatly exaggerated – especially for the smarter shopper.

APACs, the clearing organisation that takes care of card transactions in the UK, reports that card fraud cost the country £292.6 million in 2000 – up 55 per cent on 1999. Sure enough, the biggest growth area was 'card-not-present' fraud, which includes most Internet abuse, and was up by 94 per cent. At the same time, however, APACs notes that despite the scary percentage growth, the actual amount of card-not-present fraud on Internet transactions is currently very low, adding up to only 2 per cent of all card fraud.

While we may be worried about giving out our details online, we are actually far more likely to encounter fraud by handing over our cards in the restaurant, pub or shop. The commonest type of fraud is what's called 'skimming,' where the details from the magnetic strip of one card are copied onto another card without the owner knowing. In the year 2000, skimming represented 72 per cent of all card fraud. My own credit card once enjoyed a spectacular spending spree in Brindisi (Southern Italy), while I was stuck in London unaware of anything amiss. It seems the most likely explanation was a corrupt shoe shop worker 'skimming' my details to create a duplicate card.

Why hesitate to type card details into the Web when we have no qualms about giving them out over the phone, or leaving a card behind the bar all night? Most of us smile benignly as total strangers bear our plastic away into back rooms of restaurants, and, of course, we all cheerfully discard our credit card slips and receipts into the rubbish bin and then leave them outside our doors.

The bad news is that it's easy for someone to get hold of our card details, and despite any Web worries you may have, it is easier by far in the 'real' world than online. The good news is that unless you, dear reader, happen to own the credit card issuer, then the chances are you don't have to worry (and if you are the card issuer then let's face it; you can afford it). So much business relies on the convenience of making remote payments, be it by phone, mail, or the Net, that consumer law and card company policies are heavily on your side. It's in everyone's interest that you feel comfortable spending, so they make sure you have nothing to fear in the unlikely event of someone else doing your spending for you.

In the case of my own card's absentee spree in Italy, I spotted all the fun I wasn't having when it was billed to me, and promptly called my card issuer. In my mind I was scrabbling together all the evidence that I hadn't left the country (were any of my friends credible witnesses? Is a lack of suntan admissible in court?) but in the event, the card issuer simply sighed stoically and took the offending items off the bill without a question. They've been doing this for years since consumer protection legislation back in the 1970s made it the card issuer's responsibility to foot the bill in the case of fraudulent purchases where the card and customer were not actually present.

AOL has long set out to be a shoppers' paradise and makes it as simple as possible by organising it all under a shopping channel (just type in the AOL Keyword: **Shopping**). As part of that, AOL has a safe shopping scheme called the AOL Promise. All AOL certified merchants must meet high standards for customer service, secure transactions and privacy protection.

| Shopping

The government is also keen to see us spend safely, and drew up a new set of Distance Selling Regulations which came into force in October 2000. Under the new regulations, your card is covered, or as the Office of Fair Trading puts it; 'If someone else makes dishonest or fraudulent use of your payment card for any form of home shopping you can cancel the payment and the card issuer must refund the money to your account.' The important thing to note there is that the terms have changed from 'credit card' to 'payment card' to include debit cards.

The new legislation also lays down the law on a code of practice for selling, including the information that the seller has to give you, and the right to a seven day cooling off period in case you change your mind. For more details of that, get hold of a copy of the DTI (Department of Trade and Industry) leaflet *Home Shopping: Your rights as a consumer* (Ref URN 00/1127)

Fig. 1.1 The AOL shopping promise ensures total peace of mine for your retail therapy.

which you can get free from the DTI Publications orderline: 0870 1502 500 or dtipubs@ecologistics.co.uk

> *To see more information about these regulations online try http:// www.dti.gov.uk/CACP/ca/work9.htm.*

Before you go mad, however, there are a few things the regulations specifically exclude. Financial services, auctions, vending machines, pay-phones, contracts for the sale of land, deliveries of goods such as food or beverages, transport, accommodation, catering or leisure services provided on specific dates are all beyond the protective umbrella of the legislation. Some of those are very important to note; auctions, for example (see **Chapter 10**), can be one of the chief sources of fraud on the Net. The combination of competitive bidding, and the red mist of bargain hunting mean that auctions are the place and time when punters do the least checking up into what they're bidding for and who they're buying it from. Fraudsters have known that for a long time; now you do too, so be careful. The other thing is that while card issuers are very good about writing off any misuse, they do so on condition that you follow the rules and report any losses or mystery purchases as soon as you notice them. That means going through your credit card statements with care, something we don't always do. If you don't spot that your card is making purchases you didn't know about, then you're going to end up paying for it.

10 Auctions

The other point is that while card companies will pick up the bill for fraud (as long as they don't think you perpetrated it), nobody but the criminal stands to gain from it so it's in all of our interests to keep it to a minimum. There are a number of things you can do to ensure that shopping online remains safer than using your credit card to pay for a curry.

The first is that, while 51 per cent of us feel that it's not safe to use a credit card on the Net, that doesn't mean that you should feel confident sending off a cheque instead. The bulk of fraud on the Net does not involve credit cards at all. In the US, Internet Fraud Watch (http://www.fraud.org/internet/intinfo.htm) reports that of the money reported lost, credit cards only came third as the means of payment. Top was the money order, representing 44 per cent of lost money, next came cheques with 31 per cent, and only then do you get credit cards at 13 per cent. If you've sent off a cheque to a fraudster then getting your money back from the bank will be like asking the Royal Mint to issue you another tenner to replace the one you gave to that bloke on the street corner. Try to stick to cards where possible and never forget the following:

Top ten tips for the savvy shopper

1 Make sure of who you're dealing with. In the real world you can get a pretty good idea of a trader by looking around their shop. In the virtual

world, look for a customer service area, refund policy or telephone numbers. In cases where the Web site is the online arm of a high street chain you can be fairly confident of what to expect (although the likes of returns policies may still differ – see **Chapter 3**). Where the shop only has an on-line presence though, it pays to make sure you know where to find them if anything goes wrong. Any decent online shop should also give you a physical address and a phone line (be wary of mobile numbers). If in doubt give them a bell, make sure they are who (and where) they say they are, and find out if you like the sound of them.

3 Those Pesky Kids

2 If you're not happy with the trader, or simply want further reassurance, then stick to the shops that are part of a Merchant Certification Programme such as AOL's Shop@AOL or the Consumer Association's Web-Trader. Sites that can show current certificates (and logos) from these schemes or appear as sites such as 'Shop @AOL have already been checked out and found to be safe and satisfactory. As well as covering the basics such as the fact that the shop is what it says it is these schemes monitor customer service levels and delivery/returns policies. Make sure the certificate is current though – *Which?* has been known to expel some very big names from the scheme in order to make them pull their socks up and re-qualify.

Fig. 1.2   The SHOP@AOL logo.

Fig. 1.3   The Consumer Association seal of approval.

3 If you're buying from a US site then check to see if other customers have been happy. One of the best places to find out about that is the Better Business Bureau (BBB). The BBB has a Web site called BBBOnLine at www.bbbonline.com which works much like the AOL/Consumer Association schemes in the UK by asking retailers to comply with a series of standards aimed at keeping customers happy. The site allows you to check retailers that have agreed, but also lists any consumer complaints that have been registered against them.

4 Keep a record of all the contact details as well as any emails you send or receive, and make a copy of the Web page that detailed what you wanted to buy (to make a copy simply go to the page, then choose the **Save As** command from the **File** menu of your browser). Make sure you have read any terms and conditions, and make a copy of those as well.

5 Check the company's privacy policy. In the UK we're covered by the Data Protection Act of 1998. That makes it illegal for a company to pass on information about you to another company without your permission. In the US there is no such legal protection; just self-regulation. Most sites state clearly that they will not pass on your information; if they don't, you're likely to end up on someone else's mailing list just because you bought something, and that can mean being bombarded with junk email/faxes. Often there is a tick box that lets you opt in or out of mailings. Take a careful look at it though, since some ask you to tick it to opt in, and some have already ticked it for you and expect you untick it if you don't want mail. Never, ever, give out your credit card number or bank details in a plain email, and be very suspicious of anyone who asks you to do so. Don't ever give out a password; not to anyone. If someone asks for your password then report the fact to your ISP.

6 Stick to secure sites (see below, *It's OK, it's encrypted*) – those that use encryption to scramble your card details.

It's OK, it's encrypted

7 Always use a credit card where possible, as you're then protected by a pact between you and the card issuer, as well as between you and the seller.

8 If you have to pay with a cheque, use registered post and remember to keep the Post Office receipt and the cheque stub.

9 Always check your bank and credit card statements carefully to look for any unexpected transactions. If you seem to have paid more than you expected, or more often than you expected, then contact the retailer at once to find out why. Human error is a lot more common than fraud.

10 In the unlikely event of phantom purchases popping up on your statement, don't worry but do make sure you call your card issuer as soon as you can to let them know about it.

It's OK, it's encrypted – technology and security

Much is made of the idea of 'secure' sites, shopping sites that are clad in computerised chainmail complete with padlock icons, incomprehensible acronyms (anyone for SSL? SET?) and satisfyingly espionage-sounding talk of encryption. Secure sites are undoubtedly a good thing, not least because they suggest that the retailer has made the effort to protect their customers, but the very best security still comes from using a credit card and sticking to the top ten tips above.

When a site is a secure site it means that any information you type in about your card or personal details is then encrypted (scrambled) before being sent to the retailer, and only unencrypted when it has arrived at their computers. That means that while it is in transit it is completely meaningless to anyone else who tries to intercept it. Secure sites usually flash up a screen telling you that this is about to happen, and a lock or padlock symbol will appear in the corner of your browser. If you are particularly observant you may also notice that the http:// part of the Web address will change to https://. If you are using AOL 4.0 or above then you will find that every shop in the Shop@AOL selection is a secure site. The technology being used here is called SSL (Secure Socket Layer) and, while the complexity of the scrambling techniques varies (hence some sites' boast of 64-bit encryption, or 32-bit encryption), the fact is that, even in its most simple form, SSL is more than enough to put off would-be hackers because it makes interception and decoding much too much like hard work.

Secure sites, then, are good things, enough so that if a shopping site is not secured, you should wonder why and think twice before giving them any details. That is not to say, however, that just because a site is secure it means that you can forget about any of the top ten tips. There are a couple of chinks in the chainmail of secure sites, the most important of which is that SSL only protects your details while in transit. Once your details are with the retailer they are unscrambled which means that would-be hackers are going to be far more interested in probing the collected information on the retailer's computer than they are in trying to intercept traffic going in and out. After all, if you wanted to rob a bank would you rifle through its post, or head straight for the vault? The little padlock on your browser isn't going to help you if the retailer leaves their own computers unsecured, nor is it any kind of guarantee that you'll get the goods or services you want.

The answer here is to make sure you're dealing with reputable outfits and preferably those that have been given the thumbs up by a monitoring scheme. Plus, don't forget that you still have the protection of consumer legislation on your side if anything untoward does happen. Technological security is a fine thing, and getting better every day, but a tool is only as good as the person using it and it's impossible to tell from a site just how good the people are behind the scenes. Smarter cyber shoppers consider encryption security to be just one of the weapons available to them rather than the complete solution.

CHAPTER

2

Windows Shopping
(Browsing)

The Web is the world's largest shop window. It has the widest range of goods from the largest possible number of suppliers from all over the globe. There are thousands of shops with millions of products and they're all at your fingertips. So why the sinking feeling? If you're anything like me it's because you don't walk around in a Born To Shop T-shirt – you're only shopping online to save time, and you go into a blind panic when presented with a choice that involves more than three options. Personally, the thought of having to wade through squillions of cyber shops in the quest for the holy deal just makes me want to make a break for the duvet. So here's the good news. You don't even have to let your fingers do the walking, you can get the Web to do the digital legwork for you.

Price comparison sites work by asking you to type in what it is you're after, then firing off requests to all the shops they know that stock your kind of product, and picking out the best deal from the responses. They do that using automated software tools that go and retrieve the information you've requested; those tools are sometimes called 'robots' which is why you may sometimes hear them referred to as 'shop bots'. Since the people who create

Web sites tend to like anything that sounds like engineering, you may also hear comparison tools referred to as 'engines'. Whatever the terms used, the idea is the same – you type in what you want and they go off and look for it. At best they have the ability to search through tens of thousands of products in milliseconds before coming back to you with the one that's tailor made for you. Best of all it's free; at least it is for you, since price comparison sites such as ShopSmart work by taking a fee from the retailers for referring potential customers to them.

That's at best. Sadly, it's not a perfect world, and it's an even less perfect World Wide Web. Price comparison sites are a Godsend, but, like the rest of us they do have their limitations. For a start, the greater part of them, including some of the best such as BottomDollar and MySimon are geared towards the US market. That means that you have all the frustrations of a site finding you a to-die-for deal with the slight hitch that it's being offered by a Ma 'n' Pa outfit in Dead Dog, Idaho, who simply don't ship overseas. Of course you may want to check out US prices, but before buying from a foreign site of any kind, make sure you're aware of the potential pitfalls (of which more later).

There is also some discussion about the way that comparison sites work. Because many comparison sites take a fee from the shops they feature, there are accusations that the subsequent search results tell you more about their own clients than about the best deals out there. The sites that charge deny that and say that the proof of the pudding is in the prices they offer, but some sites don't take a fee specifically to avoid that accusation. There are also different ways of searching so that some sites will only look for the exact brand and product you say, where others take the approach that you probably couldn't care about the name on the computer case as long as it has an identical spec. Plus there's the thorny issue of shipping, because not all comparison sites check the postage price, which means that some online shops can catch your eye with great prices but recover some of it in mysterious 'handling' charges.

And the answer to all of these conundrums? Simple, just use lots of them. Always get a second opinion because while they go a long way towards making life simpler there's a very good chance that by shopping around just a little bit more – and that might only mean one more comparison site – you'll get an even better deal and with it the chance to be even smugger when the 'how much did you pay for that?' conversation kicks in.

Some UK price comparison sites

Price Guide UK – www.price-guide.co.uk

Price Guide claims to be the largest UK price comparison site with 250,000 price comparisons to be had.

ShopSmart – www.shopsmart.co.uk

A hundred or so shops you can grill for best prices on the kind of things you'd expect (books, games, CDs …) but also a few less common consumer categories from outdoor wear to underwear.

Fig. 2.1 Price comparison engines mean you can check every other shop's offers in one go.

Buy – www.buy.co.uk

A great site for those longer lasting consumer commitments. If you're thinking of changing Gas or Water supplier, looking for the credit card with the best APR, or trying to find the best mobile phone tariff for the way you talk then take a look at Buy. Clearly laid out, the site steps you through the key questions that you need to ask yourself before coming up with recommendations.

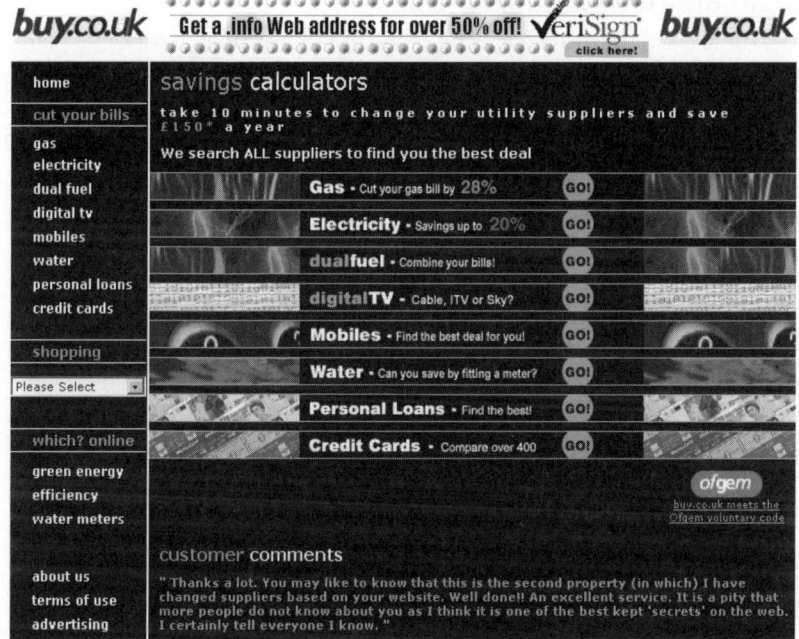

Fig. 2.2 Buy.co.uk is just one of a number of price comparison engines that find the cheapest prices for you online.

Kelkoo – www.kelkoo.com

Kelkoo is based in Paris, hence the name which a dreadful play on the French 'quel coup' (meaning 'what a find' in this case) but the company operates across nine countries and is a useful place to find European deals. Every two weeks they test their own prices and if they can find it cheaper somewhere else they invite that shop to join the scheme.

Pricescan – www.pricescan.com

Pricescan is one of the sites that makes a point of not charging a fee for listing shops, and claims to be more impartial for it. Another thing Pricescan does differently is allow you to search for something 'functionally equivalent', which makes Pricescan worth a visit for those dedicated fashion-defiers who spurn brand awareness as long as the product does the job.

DealTime – www.dealtime.co.uk

DealTime claims to browse a wider range of products than most other comparison sites, and certainly other online businesses seem to believe it. You'll probably find yourself using the DealTime search engine without knowing it as a number of other sites have done deals to use the same engine including AOL, Ask Jeeves, and the *Guardian* newspaper's Guardian Unlimited sites.

LetsBuyIt – www.letsbuyit.com

Best known of all the group buying sites – you may recall the adverts in which large numbers of ants manage to erect a flagpole. The idea behind group buying is that you want a certain car/CD player/asparagus steamer and so do hundreds of other people around the country. By coming together online you can demand and get a wholesale price, so before buying on your own take a look at what savings you'd make if you put a little teamwork on the case.

CoShopper – www.coshopper.com

Just to prove that LetsBuyIt.com isn't the only group buying site in town. CoShopper is very simple to use – you join the club by registering online (there's no charge or commitment) and then place your demand, and as soon as enough like-minded bargain hunters have done the same, your demand is automatically placed as an order with the supplier.

And some US sites

It can be an eye-opener checking the same products on US and UK sites. Of course if they do offer overseas shipping then you can benefit from the deals too, but before you do so make sure you read to the end of this chapter.

My Simon – www.mysimon.com

Crazy name, crazy site. Actually, My Simon is a really useful shopper's resource, if a bit relentlessly cheery. Easy to use and featuring a wide range of goods in its price comparisons it also includes consumer reports on all sorts of stuff from dishwashers to DVDs, many of which are equally relevant to those of us on this side of the Atlantic. It's very proud of the fact that the consumer reports go back to 1936, though for the life of me I can't see

Fig. 2.3 A US price comparison engine and the quickest way to see what you pay more for in the UK.

who'd want to read a consumer report on a consumer durable that predates WWII.

Bottom Dollar – www.bottomdollar.com
Proof positive of Basil Fawlty's assertion that everything is about 'bottoms' in the US, though rest assured the site is about lucre not lust. One of the biggest price comparison engines in the US, and the one with possibly the largest range of goods to browse through.

Buy Buddy – www.buybuddy.com
Another Uncle Sam special, particularly good for high-tech equipment. Just bought a computer in the high street? Take a look at the prices for the same kit at Buy Buddy. And weep.

Cyber shopping in the high street

Of course there are some things that we all prefer to see and touch in the flesh before we fork out. Clothes, furnishings, and other matters of taste are best perused or pawed in person, rather than glimpsed as a tiny picture on a computer. Even then the Net has its part to play. When EasyJet founder Stelios Haji-Ioanou started his chain of EasyEverything cyber cafés (which he is renaming easyInternet cafés), he imagined them as part of the high street shopping experience. EasyEverything cafés were deliberately sited on or near shopping high streets so that shoppers could take the weight off their feet with a little general surfing, and check out prices online for the goods they'd just been lusting after in shops and showrooms. The idea was you might use a high street to settle on the thing you want, but you could then go online to buy it at reduced cost.

It's a great idea, and pretty soon it had been taken one step further by companies who realised that many of us already have an even more convenient way of accessing the Web sitting in our pockets.

WAP (Wireless Application Protocol) is a technology that allows a mobile phone to display information from the Web. It's had a bit of a rough time in the press, mainly because it was originally marketed as the Web on your phone, which would only be true if your expectations of the Web were limited to black and white images on a screen the size of a postage stamp. On the other hand, that kind of display is just perfect for simple information such as pricing, which has led companies to realise that WAP turns a mobile phone into a powerful shopping tool. Just find what you want in a shop, then ask your phone if it can find the same thing for less on the Web. Companies such as Digital Rum (www.digitalrum.com) came up with the technology and started to do deals with mobile operators (such as Virgin Mobile) to give shoppers phone access to databases of available goods and prices.

American for a day

One of the things that becomes clear when using price comparison sites is that so many of the greatest deals are to be had overseas. The US is the obvious source of bargains, but shopping *sans frontières* means that it's hard not to notice that some goods are simply cheaper on the continent, or even in countries such as South Africa. So what's to stop you taking advantage of that?

In some cases, the answer is very little, but in others the savings may come at the cost of useless goods. Before comparing prices on anything abroad, it's important to make sure that you really are comparing like with like. Johnny Foreigner doesn't always do things the way we do.

For a start, there are issues of standards. Different countries have different power supplies so while there's little problem in slapping a UK plug onto something it's worth checking that it's going to be happy to sit there and feed off UK voltage. Some other countries have perversely opted for TV standards which are not the same as our own. Many modern video players can play both the European NTSC standard and the true Brit PAL but will simply sulk if confronted with an American tape. Check that there is a PAL version on offer before you even think of comparing prices.

In some cases national differences are enforced not by technical standards but by business interests. A DVD is a DVD is a DVD, but a Hollywood studio decided that it didn't want a DVD release in the US to mean that the DVD was available anywhere in the world. So DVD players are 'zoned' to make sure they can only play the DVDs that the studios intend for them. In theory, that means that if you bought a European DVD player, it won't be able to read the DVDs from zone 1. Zone 1, by the way, is the US.

Language can also be an issue. You might think that buying continental is chic and cosmopolitan but are you quite sure that you're going to be able to read the instructions, or the help files and menu options in software. Remember that if something goes wrong you may not want to be on the blower to a call centre somewhere in Albania. Which brings us round to the real biggy. Warranties.

Some warranties specify that repairs have to be done in the country where you bought the product. Others, especially those in the US, are invalidated altogether if you buy in Manhattan but live in Milton Keynes. Whilst there are such things as third party warranties available for many products, you'll have to do a little research, make sure that you can get one for your intended bargain, and add the extra cost of that to the tempting price tag being popped up by Bottom Dollar.

Of course some things, notably books and clothes, don't usually come with a lot of warranty worries. Here you mainly have to remember the postage/shipping costs and add that to the bottom line before you buy. Often the difference between US and UK prices is such that you wonder why you'd ever buy in your local high street again, until the goods actually arrive, that is, and with them comes an unexpected surprise.

Duty

Fig. 2.4 But be careful that buying 'cheaply' abroad doesn't turn into a headache on shipping and customs duty.

By and large, leaving aside the exceptions of tobacco, alcohol, and perfume, you can import goods worth less than £18 without having to worry about duty or VAT. Strictly speaking, that £18 figure should also include postage and packing. Anything over that and you have to start taking into account duty and VAT. Some items are free of both, food and books being the best example. Most items, however, manage to incur VAT (at 17.5%) and duty which seems to be calculated by taking the type of item, its declared value, and then adding a percentage based on a combination of the tax man's birthday, the phase of the moon, and the plight of the zloty.

Exaggeration? Flippancy? Hysteria? Well, judge for yourself by taking a look at the official table of duty tariffs to be found at the Customs and Excise site (www.hmce.gov.uk/). Among the gems you'll find there are the facts that shirts incur 12% duty, but outer garments are taxed at 13%. Undergarments only incur 6.5% so it's advisable to save money by moving down South where the weather's better. Plastic construction sets entail a duty of 4.7%, but wood ones rate 4.5%. Sunglasses will cost you 2.9%, CDs come in at 3.5%, but lipstick is free.

All of which means that a law abiding citizen, when out bargain hunting on the Web, will take the price being offered, convert that to sterling, and presuming that it's over £18 they will then look up the duty due, add on that percentage, then add on 17.5% VAT (where applicable) to arrive at the final cost. Got that? Good. Hardly surprising then that most people just buy online, keep quiet, and hope that Customs and Excise is too busy to notice their package of CDs. Instead what normally happens is that the sender puts a label on the outside of the package declaring the type of contents and the value, and as well as the risk of running into trouble with C & E, you may also find that the Post Office charges you a few pounds for the privilege of collecting the duty. All of which is worth bearing in mind when comparing prices abroad.

3

Those Pesky Kids

There are two kinds of shopping for kids. Shopping where you spend your money on the kids (this often carries on until their early thirties), and shopping where the kids spend their own money. In either case, the chances are that it's still your money being spent, so if there's any way of saving a few shillings in the process then that will be a small but welcome relief for parents. Since the Web cuts out the middleman, the savings can be considerable, and online shopping often comes more naturally to kids than to their parents, especially when it's their parents that pay.

Toys

Buying for baby

Lloyds TSB estimates that in the first year of parenthood you're going to spend £1,750 on bringing up baby. Which shows that they already have all the good Web addresses and have trimmed the costs down because everyone else I know seems to end up spending about that much on the first buggy. For anyone looking to find out what's available, and compare prices without wasting

Fig. 3.1 Not sure what to buy for birthdays? – just type 'Toys' for AOL's answers.

precious time charging around from one out-of-town shopping supercentre to another, here are a few suggestions of sites that can help you out at a time when you can do with all the help you can get.

Baby care is one area where it's not just a question of money. Unless you happen to live somewhere self-consciously chic you may find that back in the real world it's a choice of Mothercare or Mothercare. Mothercare exists online too, at www.mothercare.com, but there are also a whole flock of smaller producers creating offbeat and individual baby care products for whom the Web is by far the cheapest way of bringing their wares to a wider audience. Plus, Web sites bring some new ideas to the party by arranging such things as toy swaps (try Ace Toy at www.toy.co.uk or Webswappers at www.webswappers.com) and information services on the latest top toys (Dr Toy in the US at www.drtoy.com or the British Association of Toy Retailers at www.batr.co.uk). Since many of us find ourselves buying toys for other people's offspring, it is good to know that online stores are also dab hands at helping baffled buyers through the maze of toys. If you have no idea what kids of a certain age are into these days then try a present wizard, such as the guide at the Early Learning Centre (www.earlylearningcentre.co.uk) and profit from a few suggestions about what's hip and what's not for today's 11-year-olds. Combine that kind of convenience with all the information that's available online to reassure nervous parents, and you have reason enough for new parents to get surfing. If you are buying for birthdays then make sure you've read the section on **Deliveries** in the previous chapter and see whether the sites offer more expensive guaranteed delivery to ensure your Bob the Builder turns up on time, otherwise it could be a case of tears before bedtime.

2 Deliveries

Mothercare – www.mothercare.com

All the stuff you'd expect from Mothercare with the benefit of a large button on the home screen that takes you straight to the savings pages to see what's going cheap right now. A very simple way to save those precious coppers.

Fig.3.2 Taking some of the pressure out of parenting with advice and products for the new born.

Babyworld – www.babyworld.co.uk

An excellent starting point for all things baby. Babyworld looks like a parenting magazine and is stuffed with information and answers to common questions but also has a shopping section including 'how to choose' guides, as well as a handy range of their own product tests. At time of writing there is a teensy catch with Babyworld as an online shop in that the shop area itself is closed for refurbishing but the site promises that it will be bouncing back with a new selection in the near future and as long as they keep to the clarity and comprehensiveness that typifies the rest of the site then it will be one to bookmark.

Nappies direct – www.nappies-direct.co.uk

There's nothing much virtual about a nappy, but that doesn't mean the online world can't help when it comes to the task. Nappies Direct is a UK site that offers Daisy Diapers – cloth nappies in various materials for those who worry about the environmental effects of disposables. As well as buying the goods, it's also a pretty good advice site on how to live with the demands of cloth nappies.

Babies 'R' Us – www.babiesrus.co.uk

You can grumble all you like about the 'R Us' approach being responsible for the decline in literacy but when it comes to buying things the R Us empire, both in the form of Toys 'R' Us and sister shop Babies 'R' Us is just one of things you have to learn to love – like 'family meals' and theme parks. Babies 'R' Us includes all of the usual safety and convenience hardware including car seats, baby swings, gates, cots, alarms; you name it, they've got it. Information, including returns policy, is all clearly laid out on the home page and there is a handy shop information page that lets you know where your nearest shop is and what its opening hours are.

Babycare Direct – www.babycare-direct.co.uk

At first glance this site looks like they saved money by sacking the designer and refusing to have any graphics. After a few clicks however it soon becomes clear that Babycare Direct is a pared-down mean machine with products organised into clear-cut categories (bathtime, safety, baby on the move, etc.) and as little clutter in between you and the products as possible. The characters on the various items are refreshingly free of Disney, instead of which old favourites like Peter Rabbit put in an appearance and I somehow doubt that A.A. Milne would have ever guessed just how many products would end up bearing the beaming features of a certain Winnie the Pooh.

The Great Little Trading Company – www.gltc.co.uk

Not so much for babies, more a toddlers-and-up kind of shop but a nice range of slightly off-beat accessories (a triplane-shaped toy shelf anyone?) including duvets, auto-fade lamps, and storage ideas for those who still try, Canute-like, to stem the growing tide of toys and general mess washing out from the bedrooms.

Urchin – www.urchin.co.uk

Billed as 'funky stuff for baby, nursery, and small kids' Urchin features some off-beat ideas (bored of yellow bath ducks, then try a 'devil duck'…) not just for the kids but also for the parents including foot spas and aromatherapy kits, not to mention the soon to be famous spotty potty.

The Early Learning Centre – www.earlylearningcentre.co.uk

This online version of the familiar high street brand distinguishes itself by having a present finder right on the home page. From there you can choose the age group of the birthday boy or girl, pick a category of pressie, a price (phew), and even a brand if it just has to be Teletubby-related, say. The site is clearly laid out, easy to use, and a blessing for time-strapped adults.

Living dolls and other toys

The Living Store – www.bearworld.co.uk

You might expect this to be teddy bear central from the address but if you did you'd be in for a big surprise that most certainly is not a teddy bear's picnic. Our old friend Winnie is here but decidedly outnumbered by the Dipsies and La Las, not to mention Han Solo, Princess Leia and extensive selections from *A Bug's Life* and *The Simpsons*.

Ace Toy – www.toy.co.uk

This is a great shopping and swapping site with new toys and classics featured, making it a fine place for the kind of mum or dad who chooses to buy a

Scalextrix or Hornby set even though the kid is still in nappies. Go there for the kids, stay there for yourself.

Doctor Toy – www.drtoy.com

Doctor Toy is a remarkable archive of top toys in just about every category from puzzles to multimedia, from soft toys to construction sets. Like Ace Toy this has enough nostalgia factor to keep adults happy (see how many of the Classic Toy top 100 you owned) along with plenty of recommendations of good toys that kids won't have tired of in less time than it took to get them out of the box.

British Association of Toy Retailers – www.batr.co.uk

Not a toy shop as such but as close to Dr Toy as you're going to get from the UK. The BATR site lists the best sellers, the trends, the crazes, and of course has lots of those 'do you remember' moments.

Smartazz Kids – http://www.smartazzkids.com

From the name you could well think this was an American site, but thankfully you'd be wrong. Thankfully, that is, because many of the US sites don't encourage overseas shipping and when they do, they usually opt for very high delivery charges. Smartazz kids on the other hand is a European site with the advantages that its prices include standard cost shipping worldwide (an express service is offered at a premium). It also has a no questions asked refund system which is a godsend when two great minds happened to have thought alike at present buying time. Smartazz features a wide and unusual range of toys, includes a Fair Trade section who prefer their kids' toys not to have been made by someone else's kids in a sweatshop, and has feedback from other toy buyers. Highly recommended.

Toy Chest – www.toychest.co.uk

Wooden toys, outdoor toys, and such tasteful items as Jelly Brains as well as a 'pocket money' section which is what used to be called 'stocking fillers' and which goes some way to proving that you can in fact buy a toy for less than the cost of a tank of petrol.

Fig. 3.3   The finest toyshop in the world vies to be the finest on the Web.

Hamleys – www.hamleys.co.uk

The one and only, Hamleys is no longer located solely on Regent's Street – it now resides on the Web where its impressive range of toys is well supported by serious stock levels so you should never have to be turned away toyless. Well, until the next craze item comes along. A good place to go for toys with a tendency to classiness and costliness – porcelain dolls etc.

FAO Schwarz – www.fao.com

The US Hamleys from Fifth Avenue, and 'the ultimate toy store', apparently. I include FAO Schwarz not as a recommendation but as a warning. You might have heard of them, might be tempted by the product range and the slick on-site animations but be very wary of US toy shops and FAO Schwarz in particular. What happens is that you'll put items in your online shopping trolley, go to the check out, fill in a lengthy account creation form, and then be told that only orders of $200 or over are sent overseas. If you haven't finished spluttering from that you can always press on and then reel in horror at the overpriced shipping fees. World Wide Web my eye – even in cyberspace it often pays to shop local.

Toys 'R' Us – www.toysrus.co.uk

Well you knew they'd be here somewhere. The chain that had English teachers grinding their teeth all over the world has an online shop in the UK and however irritating the corporate image and logo may be, it's easy to forgive in return for a good range of toys at decent prices. A good place to go if you know exactly what you want, but not as helpful as it could be in that there is no gift suggestion engine or feedback from other buyers.

Fig. 3.4   The spelling may be suspect but you can't argue with the pricing.

4 Mil Models – www.4milmodels.com

Arguably one for parents rather than kids, 4 Mil Models is home to the modern tin soldier – all those die-cast figures and tableaux, both military and civilian.

Out of the Hat – www.outofthehat.co.uk
Puzzles, jigsaws, and pub games – toys that require just a smidgen of thinking.

UK Joke Shop – www.ukjokeshop.com
Long live the whoopee cushion, exploding cigarette, and revolving bow tie – toys that don't require even a smidgen of thinking.

JCB Works – www.jcbworks.com
Do your kids go gaga every time they see a monstrous yellow machine holding digging gear aloft? Then take a look at this official JCB shop selling toys, children's clothes, and items for grown-ups.

As well as the above specialists there are also a number of worthwhile kids departments tucked away in online department stores. Amongst those worth a look are:

John Lewis – www.johnlewis.com
The original 'never knowingly undersold' department store has a fine toy department complete with the latest offerings but also distinguished by some quality toys with an old fashioned feel such as Bow-Tie Teddies and Victorian style rocking horses.

Argos – www.argos.co.uk
The Argos catalogue has a kids' section which is helpfully broken down into a number of options from Bedroom Essentials to Outdoor Fun. A good source of reasonably priced swings, trampolines, and slides.

Littlewoods – www.littlewoods.co.uk
Littlewoods home catalogue (Littlewoods Extra) covers the range from action figures to video games, promising 'top toys that won't break the budget'.

Shopping by kids for kids

Ever tried to guide a child past a toyshop while hoping they wouldn't notice it? Some chance, and the same applies for the Web. As kids swap tips on the

Fig. 3.5 The Argos catalogue has all the good value goods you'd expect from the shops, but without the fuss of filling in the forms with those fiddly little pens.

latest must-have games and toys, they will inevitably pass on URLs and if your kids have Web access then it's as good as letting them loose in the world's biggest toy shop. As much fun as it is to drag mum and dad around and then turn to them for money, there comes a time when kids want to do the shopping for themselves. For parents, however, there are natural concerns about letting the young ones loose on the Web, and those concerns become even more pressing when there's money involved. Not least since the commonest form of payment on the Web is by credit card, and unless your eight year old sports a platinum Visa already, then you've got problems.

In the States there are services such as RocketCash (www.rocketcash.com) which seem to be the perfect solution – you set up an account for your kid(s), charge it up to an agreed sum using your credit card (which means you're still protected in the event of online fraud), and then the kids can spend that amount at online shops taking part in the scheme. The kids don't get your credit card details – all they have is the password and ID that says they have the right to dip into the agreed sum. They can't spend any more than the level you've agreed – once they've spent it that's it, and the kids haven't entered into any credit agreement so they can't get overdrawn. Perfect you might think. So where's the catch? The catch is that at time of writing, these are a largely US phenomenon. As Internet usage rises, however, more and more companies will get on the bandwagon and cross the Atlantic, so keep an eye out for it.

In the UK at the moment, the choice of shopping schemes for kids include a couple of different approaches. One is a pre-paid card, working on much the same principle as a pay-as-you-go mobile phone. The other, from Switch, is a debit card featuring greater security so that more stores accept it online (at the moment the majority of online shops opt for the safer option of credit cards).

Splash Plastic – www.splashplastic.com
A pre-paid card for those who want to shop online but are too young to have credit cards. It works just like a pre-paid mobile – you pay a sum at a shop that does 'top-ups' and that amount is credited to your account, then you use the card instead of a credit card when shopping. It can't be used to run up debts

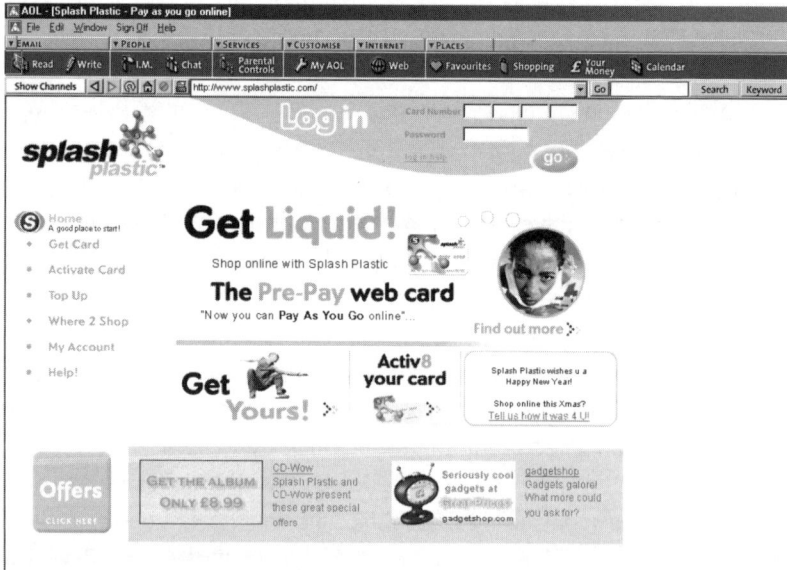

Fig. 3.6 The pre-pay shopping card for teens.

as there is no credit or borrowing involved – if the kids don't have enough money pre-paid on the card they can't buy the goods, simple.

Smartcreds – www.smartcreds.co.uk

Smartcreds is a pay-as-you-go system. Users pay money into a Smartcreds account and use the account to purchase goods online. It's a little like owning a credit card, but, unlike a credit card, you can only pay out what you've put in – there's no risk of overspending, no age restriction, and no need for a credit check. There is also no fee for joining or using Smartcreds. You can buy Smartcreds at Post Offices or Paypoints. For more information, check out www.smartcreds.co.uk.

Solo card – www.solocard.co.uk

The secure debit card from the people who gave us Switch and often seen in teenage online shops. The idea of Solo is that, just like Switch cards, Solo cards are swiped through the shop's terminal, but with Solo, each and every transaction is sent to the card issuer for authorisation, as well as to check for lost or stolen cards. Once the card issuer has confirmed that the cardholder has sufficient funds in his account, the transaction can proceed. According to Switch, nearly half a million UK outlets now accept the card.

And while you're at it take a look at:

Shopsolo – www.shopsolo.co.uk

Not the official site of the Solo card, but a portal bringing together teen oriented sites that accept the Solo card, includes fashion, games, etc.

With older children you should let them know why it's not a good idea to send off cheques or postal orders to someone asking for money. If you've read **Chapter 1, Safe Shopping** *you'll know that credit cards offer far greater protection, but if you don't pass that on, your kids may well be sending off their money to less reputable traders simply out of frustration at not being able to use a credit card option.*

1 Safe Shopping

In the meantime, the first thing to think about with kids and online shopping is that they may already be able to do it using your own cards. Think how many slips of paper are lying around the house with all your card details on them. Armed with just one credit card slip, a child can go to a site, claim to be an adult, and buy to their little heart's content or your credit limit, whichever comes first. Partly this is an education issue for your household; entranced by the magic number you use to conjure up products, children may be only too happy to perform the same trick.

To a certain extent this is also a security issue – never keep your credit card details stored on your computer and try not to leave card slips lying around. The most important thing is to keep track of your own credit card records – many kids have been able to rely on the fact that we barely bother to glance at monthly statements. If you've been using an online department store, for example, it may take eagle eyes to detect that one more purchase from that store has been slipped in there. It pays to check.

The good news is that if you find your kids have bought something you don't want them to, you're covered by the seven-day cooling-off period (presuming you find out within seven working days). Many companies have also proved very understanding about phantom purchases within the family, and may be happy to accept returns in return for continuing good will. Don't forget, though, that while you are always covered for fraud and misuse when using a card in the UK, you may not want to have to signal to a card issuer that the fraud or misuse came from within your own four walls.

C H A P T E R

4

Travel

Online travel is fast becoming a fact of life. The NOP Research Group found that almost half a million people in the UK bought their holidays online in the month leading up to the Christmas 2000. As for future predictions, Forrester Research reports that the online leisure travel market is set to represent some 14 per cent of all leisure travel sales in the UK by 2005. To do that it will grow from some £592 million now, to a healthy £3.7 billion by 2005, of which nearly half will come from online flight sales. The tragic events of 11 September, 2001, have knocked that industry back a step, but one of the side effects of the hit taken by the big national carriers is that the smaller no-frills flyers are in the process of expanding their networks; for example, easyJet's rapid growth and Ryanair's move into Frankfurt. Since they work on low margins, these cheap and cheerful carriers are very keen on cutting overheads, including booking costs, so you're more likely to see their offers online. Indeed with easyJet now nearing the figure of 90 per cent of its bookings being done online, that may well soon be the only way to get the best deal.

So why is online travel so popular? There are a number of outstanding reasons. The first is the fact that it gets away from the familiar phenomenon of the travel agent's window. You must have encountered this one: the travel agent has a board in the window just packed with exotic destinations and dream getaways at back-of-a-lorry prices. So you pop in and ask about them only to find that they have either gone or involve dates you couldn't possibly make. As soon as you say which dates you wanted to travel, the price miraculously doubles. Just to add insult to that injury we all have at least one friend who just showed up with their passport and managed to get that last minute deal of two weeks in Spain/the Caribbean/the Crab Nebula for nine pounds fifty including tax. Funny how whenever we turn up and ask about anything last minute, we get the superior smile and a brief lecture on the blessings of advance booking.

Online still has breathtaking deals aimed at those people who keep a toothbrush in their pen pocket, the difference is that we all know where to go to find them (www.lastminute.com for a start). As for the travel agent's window, you can forget the traditional disappointment because the big booking sites are arranged so that if you put in your destination and dates, any lip smacking deals that pop up are applicable to you – all you need to do is keep on clicking until the deal is done.

Doing your research

Online travel is one of the great online success stories because it brings together everything you need to know to make up your mind and sort out your holiday all without so much as a single phone call. Rather than wade through brochures and guide books trying to find a destination, you can summon them all to your screen with a mere click of the mouse. It means that you can have suggestions of destinations emailed to you, or browse a list of the latest bargains safe in the knowledge that if the price for a getaway to Tashkent sounds right, but you've lost your schoolboy diary and can't remember what country it's in, then you're only a click or two away from enlightenment.

Amongst the better onscreen travel guides you'll find several that aim to turn foreign cities into firm friends. These include Time Out (www.timeout.com)

where the Time Out Cityguides have now blossomed into one of the best online resources for urban travellers – restaurants, hotels, things to do, places for the kids – you name it, they've got it. For the more adventurous traveller in Europe, there is also Cityvox (www.cityvox.com), a multilingual travel guide to over 40 European cities and Fodor's (www.fodors.com) which has an excellent hotel and restaurant index, as well as an extensive travel forum where fellow travellers can swap notes or lose themselves in the depth of a wide range of features and articles.

> Travel Magazine

Of course, the whole point of your holiday may be to get away from the big city, in which case the more adventurous may want to head off to Lonely Planet (www.lonelyplanet.com), where the bible of the backpacker swaps its customary dog-eared pages for the Web. Ecotravellers can find out more about what they can do to ensure their holiday destination will be just as unspoilt in years to come at Ecotravel Magazine (www.ecotravel.com). Meanwhile, lovers of luxury and culture holidays are catered for at Concierge.com (www.concierge.com), a travel supersite incorporating *Condé Nast Traveler* magazine and covering a wide scope of destinations, activities and new ideas. On AOL, the shortcut to far flung daydreaming is to type in the AOL Keyword: **Travel Magazine** which pops up a travel channel stuffed with news, features, fellow travellers' tales, tips, advice and a seductive selection of holiday competitions. If you think you like the sound of somewhere, but you never paid too much attention in geography lessons and can't recall if it's an island or a capital city, then key in World Guide and help is at hand. From the World Guide you can select a country from any continent and be served up with an instant crib-sheet detailing all the essential info. Environment, history, economy, culture, the best time of year to visit, how to get there and get around, activities, visa requirements, and links to any relevant government sites are all pulled together into the World Guide.

Bargains bang to rights? So book 'em

A few tips about booking online. Online bookings are much cheaper for the holiday companies and so to encourage them they typically offer cheaper

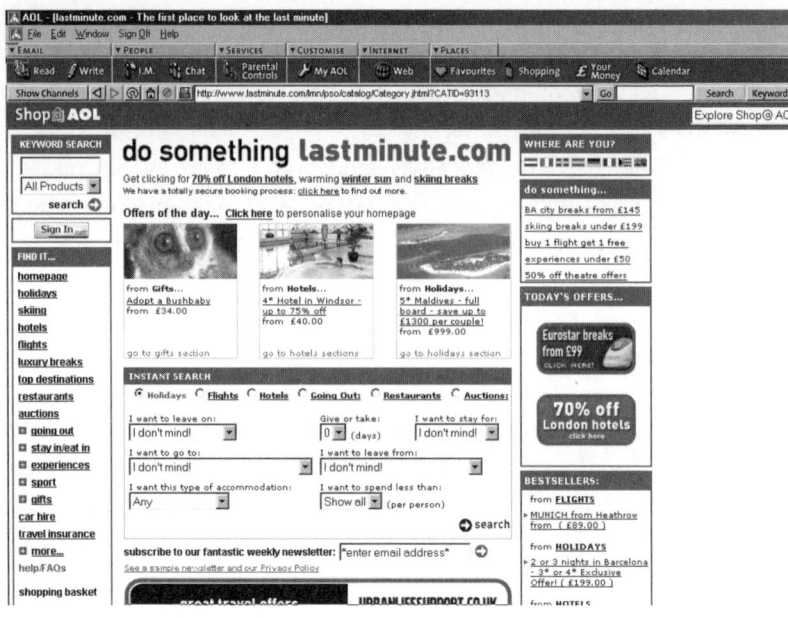

Fig. 3.7   Turn your lack of planning into inspired spontaneity.

prices or some kind of reward such as vouchers or double air miles. Anyone who's ever used a computer will be more than happy to tell you that it's not unknown for the little digital darlings to crash, and that sod's law dictates that this will happen just after you've entered your credit card details and hit the button but before you could get any kind of confirmation. In which case, reach for the phone number to get your confirmation but make sure you insist that you are still eligible for your online bonus, because even though you have ended up coming through to their switchboard, it wasn't your fault. Besides you're certainly not going to want to lose that bonus in return for the pleasures of their phone queue.

As with buying anything online you are actually covered by both the law and by the credit card companies in the case of fraud. If you're buying through an AOL endorsed trader you've also got the security of knowing that AOL will pick up the bill if you are swindled and your card company refuses to pay up for the full amount (subject to your full compliance with AOL instructions and guidelines). Nonetheless the common sense rules still apply. Firstly, make sure you know who you're dealing with and how you can contact them in the real world. Secondly, don't enter credit card details unless the detail entry page of the site is secure (whatever browser you use it will tell you if it starts a secure session with a little icon of a lock or a key). Thirdly, keep a record of your details including confirmation numbers and emails.

Cyber-savvy shoppers also know that it pays to compare pricing carefully – 'discount' famously does not mean the lowest price, and some cheaper flights manage to cut that cost by flying to airports that are not usually considered to be the obvious choice for your city destination. It's very easy if you don't know your way around a foreign city to accept that 'such and such' is the name of the nearest airport only to find that it isn't and the taxi ride will cost you the best part of your saving on the discount ticket.

Used properly, the Web is a fabulous research tool, but the Web is firmly attached to the cynical commercial world we all inhabit, so never presume that search engines are unbiased or exhaustive. Many online booking engines allow you to hold a booking for a period of 12 or 24 hours before you have

Fig. 3.8   Still the guide to big city dwelling and ideal for those weekend breaks.

to make your mind up and show your money – feel free to use that facility to reserve a deal while looking for something better. Be aware, however, that all this does is hold the seat, not the fare, so there's no guarantee you'll get that same great deal when you go back the next day.

Don't forget that flying is just a part of your travel expenses and that discounts on accommodation, taxis, car rental, and even theme parks, meals and show tickets are all available online and are all discounted in much the same way.

Flights

Bearing all the above in mind, and having decided that Antananarivo is the destination for you, all you have to do is book it. On AOL that's a simple matter of using the AOL Keyword: **Flights** and then typing in your dates and destination. After that, the engine scurries off and ferrets through the best prices it can get from the airlines before coming back and proudly presenting you with its finds. If it offers a price it's because it's available – there are none of those blackboard special disappointments because it turns out you have to travel on a Sunday and return the day before in order to qualify. By and large, such online systems, including the likes of Travelocity (www.travelocity.com) and Expedia (www.expedia.co.uk), will also return a price that is cheaper than the one you'd get if you walked into a high street travel agent. The reason for this is simple. For years now, the air travel business has been run behind the scenes by a handful of computerised booking services such as Sabre, Amadeus, WorldSpan, and Galileo. When you walk into the travel agent or call them on the phone, all you're doing is getting them to query the computer system for you. By switching to just you inputting details into the Web, the system cuts out that key-punching middleman, which means that there are savings to be made. UK no-frills carrier easyJet came to the conclusion a few years ago that in order to fill a jet on a short haul European trip, the cost of mounting the telesales operation amounts to nearly twice the price of the fuel. The cost of booking on the Web is a fraction of that and so even if they split the difference with the traveller, or provide incentives by offering double the air miles for Web-booked flights (as United Airlines has done) they still save money while offering ever more competitive pricing. EasyJet has proved keen to put its money where its mouth is, so much so that it now claims to sell

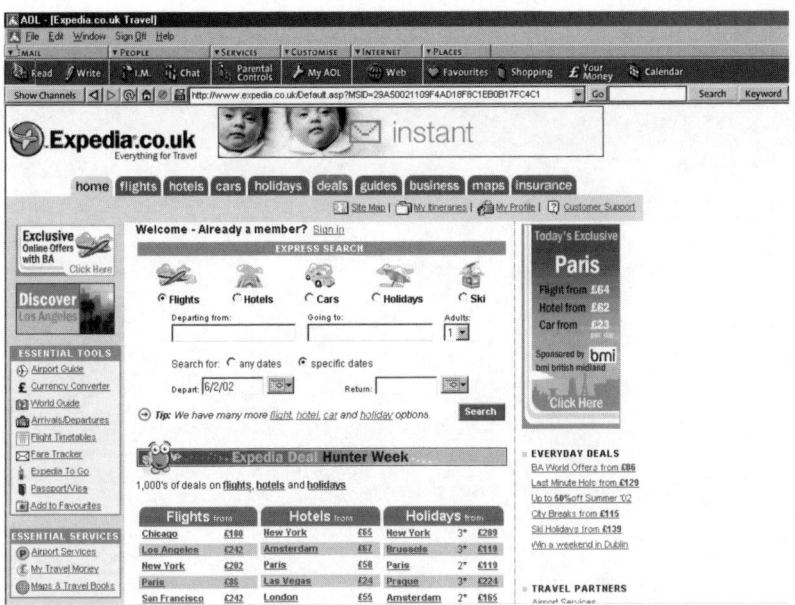

Fig. 3.9 Hard to beat for prices to the US plus loads of information to help you hit the ground running.

over 86 per cent (and rising) of its flights online. If that trend continues then such cheap flights may well become the exclusive preserve of the Web which, on its own, provides a pretty compelling reason to go online. One thing to remember though is that none of the no-frills flyers sell their tickets through travel agents, so if you want to check their cheap offers (Ryanair for example delights in offering occasional £9 one way tickets to mainland Europe), then you'd best be prepared to rummage through their individual sites. Good starting points are easyJet (www.easyjet.co.uk) which flies from Luton throughout Europe and Ryanair (www.ryanair.com), which made its name flying London to Dublin but now services very cheap and often lesser known destinations across Europe. Not to miss out on the action, a number of the bigger airlines promptly got into the no-frills market including British Airways which launched Go (www.go-fly.com), KLM UK which relaunched itself as Buzz (www.buzzaway.com) and Richard Branson's Virgin group which launched Virgin Express (www.virgin-express.com). The no-frills flyers tend to cut costs to the bone not just by selling on the Net, but by abandoning that 'free' meal

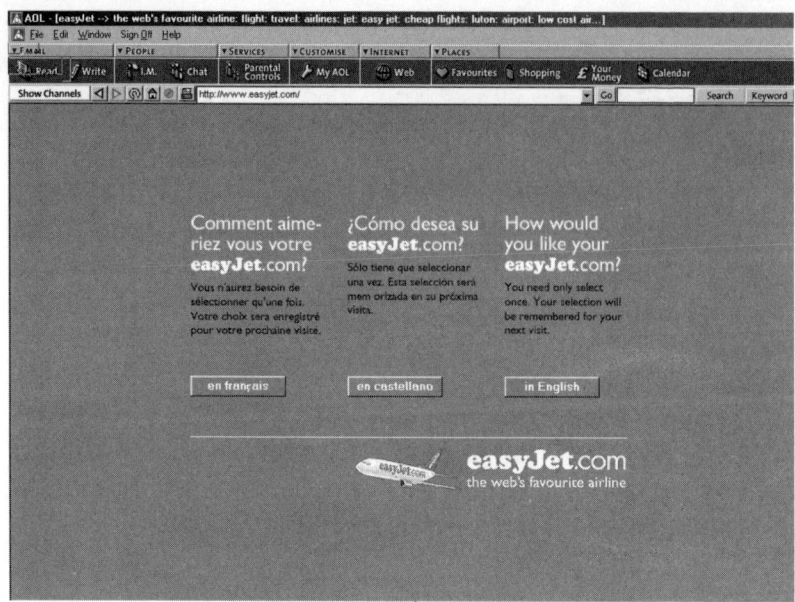

Fig. 3.10   EasyJet, the Web's favourite airline sells nearly 90 per cent of its seats online.

we all complain so bitterly about, and turning the planes around very fast indeed. This in turn often means no allocated seats – so you just turn up and pile on like a bus – and no tickets; instead you get an email confirmation and you simply quote that on arrival at check in.

Shopping around is part and parcel of buying a cheapo ticket, but it still pays to look at more than one booking engine if you're going to fly with the mainstream airlines. The problem is that many have better relations with some airlines than they do with others, which can affect both the range of prices they offer and also their destinations. Take for example the arrival of Orbitz (www.orbitz.com). Orbitz claims to have established relationships with more than 40 other air carriers, hotels and car rental companies so as to give consumers a greater choice than ever. Orbitz will hopefully up the ante with the likes of Expedia and Travelocity to introduce a Web price war. Orbitz, however, is the joint brainchild of five of the biggest US airlines: United, Continental, Delta, Northwest and American Airlines. That means that Orbitz, like Expedia and Travelocity may well have the best deals for transatlantic flights, but can't display the no-frills budget buys flying into Europe, and are often beaten by specialist bucket shops when it comes to more exotic flights into African or Asian destinations. Perhaps because our tastes and destinations differ from those of our US cousins, you may also find it repays the visit to take a look at home-grown talent such as eBookers (www.ebookers.com) and Thomas Cook (www.thomascook.com). There are also sites that don't actually sell flights and holidays but help you search and compare the online offerings. Try Cheapflights (www.cheapflights.co.uk) for example – a site that's worth the visit just for the deal of the day.

Hotels

On the accommodation front, try AOL Keyword: **Hotels**. It's always worth a sneaky peak at LateRooms (www.laterooms.com), which is a late availability clearing house for hotels and holiday rooms, and if you're off to the US then Hotel Discounts (www.hoteldiscounts.com) could well repay the effort of typing it into the browser.

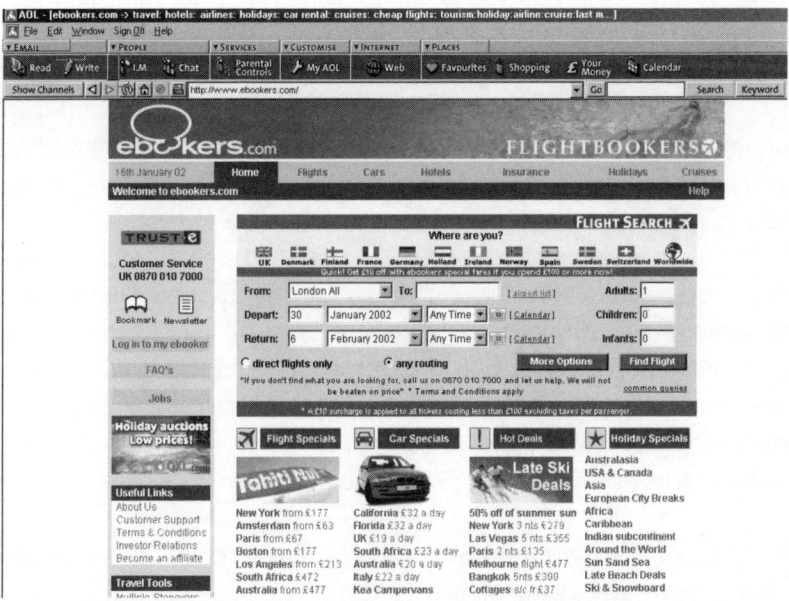

Fig. 3.11 EBookers will find that cheap flight or package holiday for you.

Last minute deals

For those in search of last minute deals try the getaways at LastMinute.com (www.lastminute.com) or the bargain basement of Bargain Holidays (www.bargainholidays.com) and/or AOL Keyword: **Last Minute Travel**.

Last Minute Travel

Price is a pretty good reason for booking your holiday online, but it's far from the only one. For a start, the chronically indecisive amongst us can revel in the opportunity that online gives us to be both choosy and confused. Not just a little bit choosy, but absolutely try-the-patience-of-a-saint picky and not simply confused but full-on clueless. Before settling on a final line up you can chop and change plans by revising routes, checking rival airlines, quizzing fares, changing dates, and seeing who caters for lacto-ovo vegetarian dog owners. The Web allows you to research the place, the geographical location, and prices from all the major airlines and a fair few you've never heard of. It never gets tired of you trying to find a cheaper route, a more complicated itinerary, or a more reasonable hour in the morning to start. Furthermore, most of the booking engines will allow you to put a hold on your flights for a day or so before you have to commit and cough up the cash. All at three o'clock in the morning. Try that with your high street travel agent.

Online sites offer more than just bookings too. Expedia, for example, has thousands of car rental deals, and hotels, usually with detailed city maps to help you hit the ground running when you do arrive at your destination. Lastminute.com features show tickets, gift ideas, and even an 'adult' section so that the amorous adventurers can order paint-on chocolate or edible underwear to accompany them on their travels. Or for around £10 you can buy an inflatable wife or husband to provide silent moral support on that gruelling business trip. Of course you might have a job explaining that one away if you're stopped at customs, but at least you can always tell them that thanks to the Web it's merely a taste of things to come in travel.

Better yet, you can turn the conventional decision-making process on its head. Conventional travel is based around the idea of you knowing where you want to go and when, but researching and booking online gives you the freedom to play with any and all of the variables. Since you're not taking up anyone's time or trying anyone's patience but your own why not try thinking out of the box a little. On a budget? Instead of looking around for something that matches the amount you have to spend why not set your own price at Priceline (www.priceline.co.uk) and see if any of the tour or flight operators are prepared to do the deal on your terms? You have nothing to lose – if nobody is interested in your offer of forty quid to go on holiday then too bad but if someone decides to take that offer rather than have an empty seat on their flight then who's laughing? Another site with an unusual take on the whole affair is Late Escapes (www.lateescapes.com) which works on a Dutch auction in which prices continue to be lowered until someone loses their nerve and snaps up the offer. Clearly this is not for those with rigid ideas about which carriers to fly with, or even specific destinations, but for the flexible traveller it can be a great money saver.

Bargains

Alternatively, you may know exactly when you're free but you're not in the slightest bit fussed where you go. In which case you might want to sign up at a service such as Travelfinder (www.travelfinder.co.uk) which will email you suggestions every day at your desk or kitchen table. If you're a subscriber then you only have to enter the AOL Keywords: **Bargains** to get some instant suggestions for getaways at prices to make you reach for your wallet. As I write there are breaks in France at £49 per week, horse riding holidays, or Salsa-learning breaks in Barcelona.

Activity Holidays

Activity holidays, incidentally, are one of the great growth areas of travel. Type AOL Keyword: **Activity Holidays** into the keyword line and adventure holidays, scuba diving, snowboarding, and cooking breaks are all presented. Whether you want to learn to Tango, watercolour, talk Tagalog, or fly an airplane, you can find suggestions that will expand your horizons, hopefully without shrinking your current account too much. The online world spans the globe and there are more things to see and do than are dreamt of in your average high street travel agency. It's not for nothing that there's a key marked 'escape' on the keyboard you know.

Research sites

Concierge.com – www.concierge.com
Travel supersite with all the *Conde Nast Traveller* magazine information and a healthy helping of *National Geographic*.

Time Out – www.timeout.com
Time Out Cityguides.

Cityvox – www.cityvox.com
Multilingual travel guide to over 40 European cities.

Fodor's – www.fodors.com
Excellent hotel and restaurant index.

Lonely Planet – www.lonelyplanet.com
Backpacker's Bible.

Ecotravel Magazine – www.ecotravel.com
For travellers with a conscience.

Holiday Ideas

AOL Keyword: Holiday Ideas
Simple way for AOL users to shortcut to far-flung fantasising.

Cheap no-frills flyers
- EasyJet – www.easyjet.co.uk
- Ryanair – www.ryanair.com
- Go – www.go-fly.com
- Buzz – www.buzzaway.com
- Virgin Express – www.virgin-express.com

Flights

Bargains

Booking sites
- Travelocity – www.travelocity.com
- Expedia – www.expedia.co.uk
- Orbitz – www.orbitz.com
- Priceline – www.priceline.co.uk
- Travelfinder – www.travelfinder.co.uk
- eBookers – www.ebookers.com
- Thomas Cook – www.thomascook.com
- lastminute.com – www.lastminute.com
- Bargain Holidays – www.bargainholidays.com
- … or AOL Keywords: **Flights** or **Bargains**

5

Finance

In much the same way as the Web takes out the middle man and puts you in the driving seat when it comes to booking holidays, the world of finance, another largely computerised affair, is a natural fit for online services. By going online, you can very quickly compare the many financial products out there, and because an online customer uses less time and resources, many financial institutions are more than happy to give them preferential rates on everything from current accounts to loans.

Online banking

Banking

A great many of us aren't actually loyal to our banks, just stuck with them by inertia. This is daft given that it's a long time since bank staff knew who you were, let alone respected you for your long custom. Most of us have current accounts that don't pay interest, and credit cards issued by the same bank that holds our current account, on which we pay interest over the odds. If you want to get an idea of how much better your current account could treat you, and at the same time how much less per month you could be paying on your credit cards, then the Web's the place to go. On AOL just type in the AOL Keyword: **Banking** or if you're not an AOL user, try the comparison engines available from Blays (www.blays.co.uk).

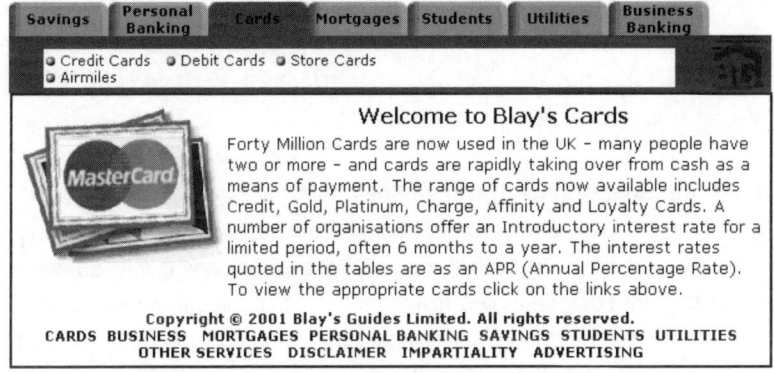

Fig. 5.1 Confused by all those competing credit offers? Let Blays cut to the chase for you.

Chances are that you'll instantly find that you can get a better rate of interest on a current account by changing to one of the leading online banks. Actually most of the best credit card and mortgage deals are also from the online banks. In part this is down to the savings they can make on not dealing with customers face to face, in part it is because the online banking area is relatively new and very competitive, but to a large extent it is simply because the customers who research on the Web are very aware of the deals out there and know they are never more than a couple of clicks away from the next one. Since the majority of online banks are backed by the big boys from the high street, it makes sense to make the most of them.

Whether you get to the Blays engine through AOL or not, you will find that if a deal catches your eye, you can link directly to them and apply online to open a new bank account, and eventually transfer money to it from an old one. At AOL Keyword: **Banking**, I find that I can get a better rate of interest on a current account by changing to one of the leading online banks. While I'm at it, I can also find out just how much I am overpaying for my credit card and mortgage. It doesn't take long to establish that just about every one of the better deals is indeed from an online bank. I can link directly to them (on AOL, just type the name of your chosen bank into the Keyword box), apply online to open a new account, and eventually transfer money to it from an old one.

In the case of credit cards this can be a joyful process since many of the cards out there not only offer better rates than those your bank has cheerfully charged you, but also offer a six- month interest- free period for balance transfers from old cards.

For those unsure of how to contact their own banks online, there is also a bank finder which will link into that bank's Web site (presuming there is one of course), or you can just type in the name of the bank and it will probably be an AOL Keyword that takes you straight there. All of this can be done without braving the elements, the queues for tills, the bank manager, or even leaving the keyboard. The fact that I can get an instant statement at any time of day or night, extend an overdraft, or pay bills all without having to deal with another person (and save money because of it) is a great benefit.

The Your Money Channel on AOL has tips and pointers for all the common banking products from overdrafts to children's savings accounts. Information from a trusted source such as the British Banker's Association (www.bankfacts.org.uk) lets you find out about how bank accounts work or how the Euro will affect you, while its currency converter is an invaluable tool when thinking about buying from abroad or going on holiday (see **Chapter 6**).

6 Entertainment and Leisure

There are a couple of things to be careful of. The first is that not all online banks are equal, and the best judge of them is their backer. If the online bank in question happens to be a solid high street name (such as Egg which is really the Prudential in disguise, or Smile which is an alter ego for the Co-Op), then all is well and good. Just because it has a '.co.uk' domain name doesn't mean it's British, however, and if you find you don't know the backing institution you may want to be wary. There has been a case of online banks stumbling, though so far their customers have simply found their accounts and money transferred to another bank, but you're going to feel a lot more secure sticking with companies you know. The other thing is that reports suggest that some people have found themselves being refused credit after moving their credit cards repeatedly to new accounts, even though they did not exceed their credit limits. This can happen because some systems date back to the days when we all stayed with our banks for life and so automatically logged it as suspicious if more than a certain number of credit checks were run on an individual in a given period. Since there is an automatic credit check whenever you apply for a new card, this could theoretically end up tagging those who simply had the savvy to shop around. Most computer systems have been updated to allow for the new, more flexible consumer, but if you suspect that this has happened to you then help is at hand online.

If cards or loans are refused there's always the possibility that you've found your way onto a credit blacklist. Should you be bumping up against financial

Fig. 5.2 All you need to ensure that you're in the best of financial health.

barriers, you may also be interested in the advice on offer from This Is Money (available on AOL or at www.thisismoney.co.uk), which will give you the low down on how to find out just what a credit blacklist is, how they are compiled, and most importantly, how to find out if you're on the wrong end of one. The all-too-likely possibility that you could be on one by mistake is considered, and there are examples of pre-formatted letters you can copy off to send to those concerned if you think that is the case or simply want to have details of what information they are keeping on you. Of course loans may actually be part of the problem, not the solution, and as well as online tips on getting out of debt, the Consumer Credit Counselling Service (www.cccs.co.uk) is at hand with discrete counselling.

If you're not in financial trouble but would like to know more about the mysterious ways in which banks work, then there is a wealth of advice available online. The Your Money channel of AOL has tips and pointers for all the common banking products from overdrafts to children's savings accounts. On the Web the British Banker's Association (www.bankfacts.org.uk) lets you find out about issues such as how bank accounts work or how the Euro will affect you, while the currency converter from the same source is an invaluable tool when thinking about buying from abroad or going on holiday.

Calculators and counselling

There's only one way to become a millionaire. Sort out your money problems and start saving. Of course, it isn't that simple, but the AOL Your Money Channel can certainly help you make a start. In fact, as a bit of fun, at Aol Keyword: **Tips and Tools**, you'll even find a millionaire calculator! Just key in when exactly you would like to be a millionaire (that would be now, surely), your current savings, and the amount you can afford to put aside each month. Hit the button and it calculates whether you will be a millionaire in time for your goal. Should you somehow fail to hit the magic figure, it suggests that you might need to consider upping your savings amount. In my case, grateful as I am for the suggestion that I increase my monthly savings by some £81,021.39, I would be even more grateful for ideas of just where to find those extra pennies.

My first step is to use the budget calculator, which can be found at AOL Keyword: **Saving**. This is relatively quick and simple, yet still light years away from the back of envelopes approach that typifies my normal monthly budgeting. After inputting my income, the budget calculator prompts for the commonest types of outgoings, including those we're often inclined to overlook, such as insurance and credit card payments. It then calculates all of these outgoings as a percentage of your incomings to help identify the problem areas.

Saving

If you're prepared to spend a little more time and effort on visualising your financial health, and that of your business, then you may find the interactive financial tools at the Insolvency Helpline (www.insolvencyhelpline.co.uk) helpful. Don't be put off by the name – you don't actually have to be insolvent to use the helpline, but if you are worried about cash flow take a look at the tools section where you will find such things as a stock turnover calculator, gross profit calculator, taxable profit calculator and an indicator of business health. In the AOL Small Business area (AOL Keyword: **Small Business**) you'll also find plenty of help if you're either already running your own business or thinking of starting one up.

Small Business

Finding loans and mortgages

Loans

Other online calculators include the FT Loan Finder which can be found at AOL Keyword: **Loans**. Loan Finder works by asking you just how much money you want to borrow, and how long for, whether you intend to offer security (i.e. against a home you own) and what your age is. On the basis of that, it polls the current rates of major lenders and comes back with the various total repayment figures that are on offer. In some cases (depending on the lender), if one of them does appeal to you it is then possible to apply for that loan there and then online via a link to the lender's site. You can check how much you can afford to borrow first though by using the loan size calculator (AOL Keyword: **Loan Calculator**).

Loan Calculator

The biggest loan any one of us is ever likely to take out is a mortgage, and it's a potential minefield for a number of reasons. Firstly, there's always the feeling that buying property is so eminently sensible – you can't go wrong with property right? Which, unfortunately, leads to the feeling that there couldn't possibly be anything wrong with stretching your borrowing just that little bit further to get a little bit more brick and mortar. AOL Keyword: **Mortgages** will help make sure you don't overstretch yourself and that you get the right deal. You can check the best offers from all of the UK's leading lenders, and find the best mortgage for you – whether you're a seller, buyer, or second-homer. There are also plenty of tips on what to look for in selling and buying property. Best of all there is a calculator so you can key in the amount you're looking to borrow and then find out what that translates to in terms of monthly holes in the joint account. It may kill the romance of house hunting a bit, but it's better to learn sooner rather than later. You can also get your mortgage or re-mortgage online using the tools and links AOL provide.

Mortgages

Pensions and other savings

For those lucky enough to have a spot of spare cash swilling around, and keen to ensure that they can afford such luxuries as holidays abroad in the future, the obvious step is to look into savings. A peek at the top ten savings accounts (AOL Keyword: **Savings**) should give you an idea of where you can get the best interest rates on savings, but that doesn't mean that your savings are free from the clutches of the taxman. Savings is an area where advice is more than welcome since trying to get to grips with the differences between a Managed Fund ISA, an Index Tracker and a Self Select ISA is not something most of us feel comfortable with. Furthermore by finding out about such things online, you don't have to face a financial advisor in front of whom you inevitably ending up nodding and smiling while secretly not understanding a word he or she is saying. Should your eyes glaze over while learning about finance online you can always take a break and try again later and that can be priceless.

Savings

If, after reading through all the advice online, you still aren't sure what would be the best for you then why not ask the experts directly? From the Your Money page, you can click **Ask the Experts** and either send off your own queries, or take a look at the questions other people have asked and had answered by financial advisors. Beating the taxman, maximising savings, choosing a pension – it's all there.

Pensions

On the subject of pensions, it's worth taking a couple of minutes to look at the calculators on the Pensions page (AOL Keyword: **Pensions**). These allow you to key in your current savings and pension contributions and see how much money you'll be earning from them on retirement. If you've already looked at the information on how little a state pension will bring you then the results of the pension calculator can make for sobering reading. Should that be the case, you can read on for further pension information to help select one that's right for you and will bring you the highest reward. Not that you have to take AOL's word for it: hear it straight from the horse's mouth at the DSS department of work and pensions (www.dss.gov.uk). The scary fact is that individuals who have both paid full National Insurance contributions would only get a full state pension £72.50 a week. Which means that if your dreams of retirement revolve around Caribbean holidays and golfing weekends you'd best start researching your pensions now.

Share dealing

Fool

Online share dealing took off in a big way simply because at last the little man could get access to the same information as the pros. That has had its

Fig. 5.3   The Motley Fool dishes out some of the wisest financial advice on the web.

downfalls, not least as inexperienced investors have often been caught out by the occasionally violent swings of the markets, but if you are interested in investments and shares there are a few things you can do that let you flutter while keeping your shirt firmly on. The first is to learn a little about how it all works, on AOL simply type the AOL Keyword: **Fool** or on the Web go to the Motley Fool Web site (www.fool.co.uk) which, despite its name, is where the wise go to find out how the whole thing works. Next you can use the Web to dip your toe into the financial waters without being devoured by sharks. To speculate on shares without any risk whatsoever, you're going to need imaginary money and a virtual portfolio. From AOL type the AOL Keyword: **Shares**, select **My Portfolio** and you're off. First you'll need to click **Create** to get a Portfolio up and running, then select **Add** to include the shares that interest you. The **Add** menu lets you pick from various international markets including the UK, Europe, and Canada, with all the familiar names from Nasdaq to Ftse. Having selected a market you can look up companies by name, or their first letter, or their symbol if you already know it and that will pull up the latest information on price and performance. From there, if you like what you see, all you have to do is select that company, enter the current share price (which you get when you look up the company details) and how many shares you fancy buying. That done, the shares are added to your portfolio and updated with the information from the markets so you can sit back and see how you would have done had you really gone ahead and made the purchase. If you feel you can beat the markets then why not try your skills at fantasy speculation against other players? There are competitive investment games such as Fantasy Trader (on the Lycos UK money page at www.lycos.co.uk/webguides/mc/pfinance/) that give you a large, if sadly imaginary, sum and set you up against other players to see who can make the most money in a given time.

Shares

Of course, if the virtual portfolio still leaves you with an appetite for risking the real thing then the Web is the place to do it. The number one in online trading is Charles Schwab (www.schwab-worldwide.com), although eTrade is also up there and has a UK site at www.etrade.co.uk, as has Stocktrade (www.stocktrade.co.uk). eTrade, incidentally, often has offers to encourage new investors, such as 30 days of commission-free trading.

CHAPTER

6

Entertainment and Leisure

If you've followed the advice in Chapter 5, you're now financially sorted and feeling flush so now it's time to blow the dough on having fun. Although the Internet started life as a military communications system designed to survive the cold war, and the Web itself was created by earnest minded scientists, you could be forgiven for thinking the whole thing was created to serve the interests of visitors from the planet fun.

Music, magazines, CDs, books

Some would say that this is what the Web does best, and whenever two people get together and talk about online shopping you know that it's just a matter of time before the name Amazon crops up. Amazon made its name for a number of reasons, many of them innovations that have now set the shopping standard. Firstly, it was (and is) cheap. Secondly, it let you know just how much you were saving on the published price so you could see that even if a book caught your eye in the shop it was often worth waiting until you were back home and at the keyboard before ordering it. Thirdly, it brought in user reviews and recommendations. Select a book in Amazon or its many imitators

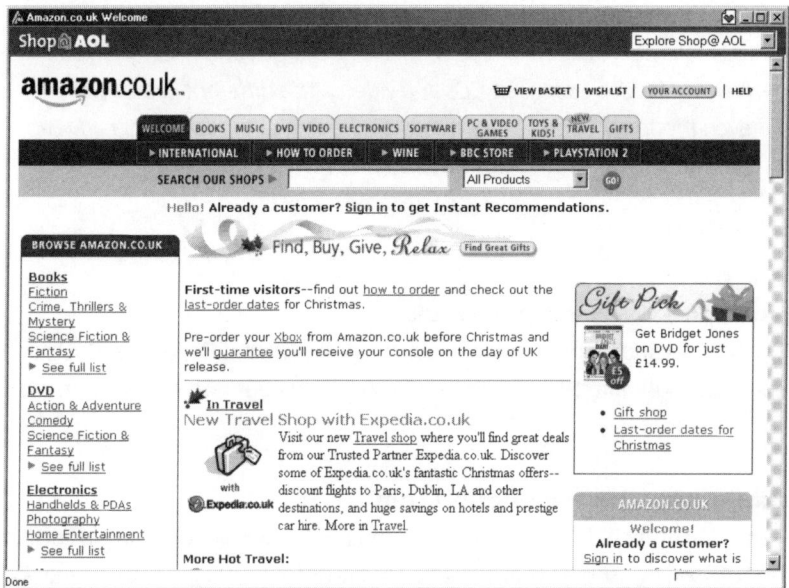

Fig. 6.1 The original and many would say still the best, the online book shop giant has now expanded into DVDs, CDs, travel, and even wine.

and you will like as not see a list of other books suggested. The list is based on books that were also bought by people who liked the one you're looking at now, so it goes beyond selling you a book and into giving you a path for further reading. Reviews not only mean you can see what others said, but also try your own hand at reviewing and tell the world why they should care about your beloved author or character. Fourthly, shopping baskets meant that you could build up a list of books you wanted and pay for them all in one go, or better yet put them to one side and wait until you were sure, or had been paid, safe in the knowledge that you selection would still be there just as you left it when you returned. CD sellers quickly caught on and joined in with the same approach. Fifth, Amazon and other online booksellers such as AOL can access a range of books beyond the wildest stockroom of the average shop. Amazon may have since had to watch while others did exactly the same, but as a consumer why should we care; the more the merrier, the winners are us. Pretty much all of the following have now branched out beyond books and into music and videos as well.

*One little thing. Books are blissfully tax and duty free in the UK, US, and Australia so just keep an eye on delivery charges and price and you'll have no hidden expenses. CDs and videos are a different kettle of taxes even though they may share pages on the same sites; for further advice see the section entitled **American for a day** in **Chapter 2.***

2 American for a day

Amazon – www.amazon.co.uk

The original and, many would say, still the best. Books, CDs, videos, DVDs and computer software all with the familiar Amazon approach and all from a UK site.

Bibliofind – www.bibliofind.com

Remember that old Yellow Pages ad with J.R Hartley looking for an old copy of his book on fly fishing? That's what Bibliofind is for – just type in the name and it links into Amazon's list of rare and second hand books to see if it can find a dog-eared old copy. Priceless if you're ever after a copy of your grandpa's favourite childhood book.

Alphabetstreet – www.alphabetstreet.co.uk

The nice thing about Alphabetstreet is that, as well as a good range, it also pays close attention to its delivery deals. At the moment it allows you to add as many items to your order as you like and still only pay £1 delivery within the UK. Considering the majority of its stock is sent out within 24 hours this is a truly great deal.

Borders

People in Britain are increasingly familiar with the huge Borders shops and the one in London's Oxford Street took over from Foyle's as the country's biggest bookshop. Typing in the Web address www.borders.com is a tad pointless, however, as all it does is link straight to Amazon.

Waterstones – www.waterstones.co.uk

Looks familiar? It should do; like Borders, Waterstones is another link to Amazon.

BOL – www.bol.com

European book superstore noted for its offers such as three for a tenner as well as substantial reductions on published rates. Shipping in the UK is £2.95 though, which can wipe out those savings so check with a price comparison engine that includes delivery cost before you buy. Bol also have a good music selection.

Tesco – www.tesco.com/books

Yup, more proof if proof were needed of the supermarket's push into just about everything you can buy. Delivery is clearly stated right from the start as £2.25 plus 50p per item and just as the supermarkets have ranges of discounted popular foods, so the bookshop promises that its bestseller list will be a guaranteed ten per cent cheaper than Amazon. Worth a look for that alone.

CDs, music, and films

The important thing to remember about music and videos or DVDs is that, unlike books, they are subject to duty if you buy them abroad. In the case of video and DVDs, they may also simply not work, since the US TV format is NSTC while in the UK we use a system called PAL. Some video players can cope with multiple formats, some can't, so it makes sense to check you can play anything back if you buy abroad. Likewise, DVDs suffer from 'zoning' imposed by the film distributors so that DVDs sold in the US have a code that prevents them being played by DVD players from elsewhere on the planet. DVDs can be 'chipped' to get around that and enable them to understand all DVDs but if you're about to buy US specials then you'll have to make sure your machine can play them. Caveat emptor, or 'buyer beware,' is the watchword here.

That point aside, music is best bought on the Web for a number of reasons. Firstly, the price comparisons between Web outlets and high street shops mean you can find great deals in split seconds. Secondly, using the Amazon-style recommendation system you can see what other people bought after the album that interests you and get tips on what you might go for as a result. Thirdly, most of the good sites allow you to listen to clips from an album there and then using streaming audio.

Streaming media, MPEGs, MP3s and other multimedia magic

Often the sites that sell sound and vision will let you download samples, either as playable video or animation files stored on your hard drive, or as streaming media. To play streaming media you either need to have Real Audio from www.realnetworks.com, the Windows Media Player (usually already installed in your Windows system), or AOL's media player if you're using AOL 6.0 or 7.0. Most sites will automatically check to see if you have the right software and if not they will link to a site where you can download it. Streaming media is like downloading a file with the twist that the player saves time by starting to play the beginning of track while it is still downloading the end of it in the background. Usually it doesn't store the file on your machine, and with a reasonable connection you just click on the play button online and the music will play on your computer (providing you have speakers or headphones plugged in of course). When the connection is very fast (what's known as 'high bandwidth') it's possible to stream enough information to deliver full screen full-motion video over a phone line or TV cable which is how some services called ADSL or Cable Internet access can deliver video on demand – though most domestic broadband packages fall short of this. Streaming media is instant, it means you pick whatever you want to hear a sample of (unlike the CDs set up for you to listen to in a shop) and unlike listening to a sample in a shop it means you never again have that vaguely uncomfortable feeling of putting on headphones that are warm and moist from someone else's ears.

Downloaded files such as MPEG (from the Motion Picture Expert Group that sets the standard for the video and audio compression used) video files mean you have to wait while the file is siphoned off the site and copies to your own computer but once there they are yours and you can play them over and over whether or not you are online. Most downloaded formats can be played on the Microsoft Windows Media player or the AOL media player and those that can't be played by the software you already have will normally point you to the site where you can get the player you need.

MP3s are music files that have achieved some notoriety. The name refers to the fact that they are the audio part of one of the Motion Picture specification of MPEG but it was soon realised the MP3 compression system was just excellent at forcing fat audio files into svelte little sizes that could be squeezed down phone lines. Immediately MP3 became the pirate's favourite as you could strip a track off a CD, compress it as MP3, and post it to the web for anyone to download and play for free. Napster became famous as the world's most popular sharing site for such files until the copyright lawyers finally got a grip. MP3s are still out there (leaving aside the word 'sex', 'MP3' is the commonest word entered into search engines), often free, and Napster's signing of licencing agreements with big business means that it will probably soon be a formal means of distributing music for money as soon as the industry works out the best way of doing this. Although you can get tiny, stylish, solid state (no moving parts like there are on CD players or tapes) MP3 players you don't have to have one to listen to MP3s – you can copy them from your computer to a Mini Disk or your computer itself will do the job for you if you download one of the thousands of players on offer.

Shops

Go to AOL Keywords: **Music Shop** or **Games Shop**. Or if you don't have AOL to hand try the following …

Music
Tickets to ride
As well as buying CDs and minidiscs, you can also buy tickets for concerts online. Some of the big outlets include lastminute.com (proving that it does do a lot more than just travel), as well as the agencies like Keith Prowse but there are also a few online specialists you may not have heard of.

Aloud
www.aloud.com
Superb ticket sales site where you can search for what's coming your way by entering the artist, the music genre or the venue then snap up those tickets pronto.

FirstCallTickets.com
www.firstcalltickets.com
Theatre, concerts, sport, exhibitions, if there are tickets to get into it then you can buy them here.

Fig. 6.2 'All the live event tickets you can buy online' and none of the queuing or touting.

Ticketmaster

www.ticketmaster.co.uk

Music, theatre, sport, performing arts, the lot. Whether your chosen stomping ground is the ENO or Elland Road this is the place to go if you want to get in.

LatestEvents.com

www.latestevents.com

Fancy travelling further afield for your pleasure? Going away for a weekend and wonder whether you can get opera or sports tickets while you're there? Well this is the place for events and gift ideas across Europe.

Lastminute.com

www.lastminute.com

No they don't just do travel, they also provide cheap deals on last minute (and not so last minute) concerts and sporting events. Of course if you want to travel to go to a concert they could also sell you a flight to go with your tickets.

Keith Prowse

www.keithprowse.co.uk

Familiar to anyone who's stayed in a chain hotel the Keith Prowse ticket empire is online, although in the UK it focuses entirely on corporate events.

Amazon

www.amazon.co.uk

Books, CDs, you name it they'll cheerfully knock something off the price and ship it to you.

Audiostreet

www.audiostreet.co.uk

Lots of sound clips, CDs, and DVDs. Audiostreet features low prices, VAT is included in those prices, and there is currently only a £1 delivery charge per order in the UK. What are you waiting for?

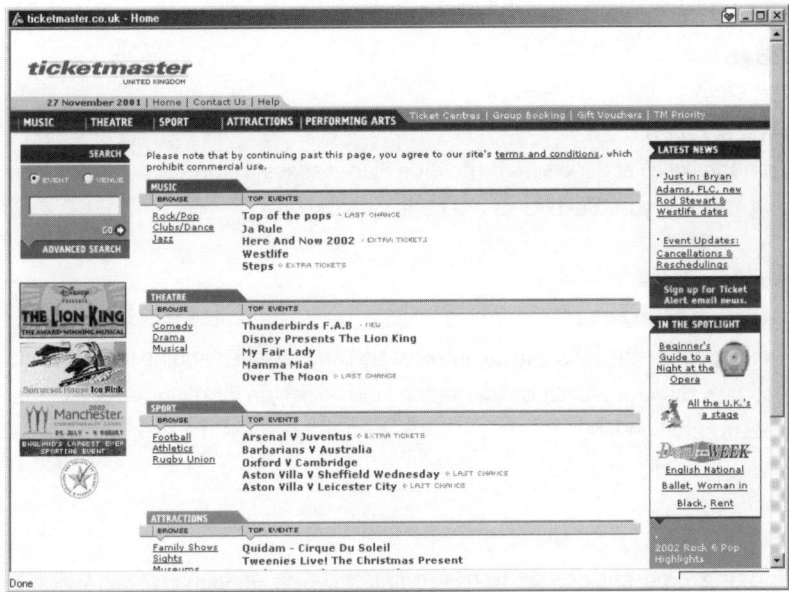

Fig. 6.3 Tickets available for concerts, but also comedy, drama, sports and all the big attractions.

101 CD

www.101cd.com

Arguably the best thing to come out of Croydon, OK I know that's not saying much but don't be put off 101CD, which may look a little less slick than the big boys but is cheap, cheerful, and smacks of enthusiasm if not actual obsession.

HMV

www.hmv.co.uk

Took a little while to get there but now safely installed online and offering prices that can't be beaten in the high street.

Ministry of Sound

www.ministryofsound.com

Clubbing scene for those who miss that hard trance Ibiza beat.

Cheap or What

www.cdwow.co.uk

Name says it all. Great prices which generally include free delivery.

Video

BBC Shop

www.bbcshop.co.uk

From the magical deep sea of the Blue Planet series to the surrealism of Ripping Yarns all your Beeb faves are here.

Film World

www.filmworld.co.uk

The film buff's site, news, trivia, information and a search engine that lets you search by director – because you're the kind of person who's interested in the maestro's full oeuvre.

Blackstar

www.blackstar.co.uk

From the Simpsons box set to the complete works of Salma Hayek, when it comes to video Blackstar simply has it all.

Games

> Games

As access speeds get faster, computer software and games in particular will cease to be something you go to the shop to buy, and will instead become something you pay for online and download directly to your machine. With software, the Web can not only be the showcase and the shop but also the shipping agent, delivering by download there and then. There are already hundreds of games and demos you can download, some free, some shareware, some tasters for professional products, and all of them the shape of things to come. The latest generation of games consoles such as Microsoft's X box also have modems built in to make use of the Net as a software supplier. Right now though most of us use a dial up connection that would take all day to download a typical commercial game, so it still makes sense to surf, buy, and then wait for the CD-ROM to arrive in the post. If you're an AOL user and you want to know what's out there then simply type the AOL Keyword: **Games** and you'll find a series of games on AOL, as well as links to reputable game sites on the Web. To buy games software and hardware, go to AOL Keyword: **Games Shop**. If you're not an AOL user here are a few places to look at games for downloading or buying (PC game sites, in addition to the book and CD sites above, most of which carry games too).

> Games Shop

Jungle
www.jungle.co.uk
Jungle is a great site for games, games consoles, and indeed just about every-thing else electronic from MP3 players to computers. As well as cheap prices galore it also happens to be the only UK Web site to offer the official merchan-dise from the Tomb Raider movie.

Simplygames
www.simplygames.co.uk
One of the most popular games sites in the UK, run by enthusiasts for enthu-siasts, and since they know you simply can't wait to get your paws on the games you've bought it sends out all software by first-class recorded delivery.

UK Games
www.ukgames.com/
Don't go to this site if you're a casual browser. There is so much here that, unless you know the games you want, you're likely to lose them in the astonishing number of titles fighting for screen space.

Game
www.game.co.uk
Exactly what it sounds like, with a wide range of games for PC and consoles.

There are also games you can download for computers which are either freeware, or shareware which normally allows a taster of a game or application but requests that you pay to get access to all the levels, or all the features. Such sites include:

PC Gameworld
www.pcgameworld.com
Yes, it's US based, but until they work out how to tax bits and bytes moving over the Web you simply don't have to care when it comes to downloads.

Download.com
www.download.com
Games are just one category of software available for download here, much of it shareware, much of it completely free, and all of it with helpful descriptions.

Computers, electronics and photography

> Shop

Before you buy anything, anything at all to do with electronics, check out the **shopping comparison engines** discussed in Chapter 2 – the variation in pricing is astonishing. Go to AOL Keyword: **Shop**, and click on Computing & Games or Electronics & Photo. Or on the Web, try the following.

> *2 Shopping comparison engines*

Jungle
www.jungle.co.uk
See above, under 'Games'.

Dixons
www.dixons.co.uk
Everything from two-way radios to wide-screen TVs.

Microwarehouse
www.microwarehouse.co.uk
Computers galore, along with printers, PDAs and software. Also familiar as
the home of the Inmac catalogue so you get to the same place if you enter
www.inmac.co.uk

PC World
www.pcworld.co.uk
You know the name, you know the snappy little jingle, now you can check out
the range without driving to that edge of town superstore.

Comet
www.comet.co.uk
Not just electronics and computers but all the consumer durables you could
shake a credit card at and a promise to beat the online prices of their rivals.

The Gadget Shop
www.gadgetshop.com
Electronics but also all those eye-catching widgets from robot dogs to port-
able fridges.

Firebox
www.firebox.com
The toy shop for the grown up kid – go to this site and you are guaranteed to
stumble across something that makes you think about your next birthday.

Then there are also the direct sales outfits which often allow you to config-
ure a computer exactly the way you want it then buy it for less than it sells

Fig. 6.4 The finest place to shop for toys for (big) boys, and indeed girls.

in the shops. If you're buying for business you may also want to try a tendering portal such as Mondus (www.mondus.co.uk) where you say what you want, and let different suppliers bid for your business. While you're at it, if you're shopping for the office you might want to take a peek at **Euroffice** (www.euroffice.co.uk), an online office products company with over 20,000 products and free delivery on orders over £30.

Dell
www.dell.co.uk

Apple
www.apple.com

Elonex
www.elonex.co.uk

Gateway 2000
www.gw2k.com

Tiny
www.tiny.com

7

Clothing, Beauty Products, Sports, and Department Stores

If you're ever after a particular product, say a brand of perfume or a certain designer label, then remember that you will probably find it just by going to a search engine such as Google (www.google.co.uk) and typing in the name. You may find it easier to go to a natural language search site such as Ask Jeeves (www.ask.co.uk) where you can type in a question like 'where can I buy Chanel no.5?' and promptly receive a series of links to sites that will be happy to take your order. If you are an AOL user you'll probably find just what you want from the Shop@AOL channel (AOL Keyword: **Shop**) which has a directory of shops and brands you can buy, all protected by the AOL promise (see **Chapter 1**). There are also sites offering good general advice such as the *Guardian's* Shopping Unlimited (www.shoppingunlimited.co.uk) and comparison sites such as 2020shops (www.2020shops.com) that keep you up to date on what's out there and whether they're any good. Another great way of keeping on top of the bargains is to sign up for shoppers' newsletters. AOL's shopping newsletter (AOL Keyword: **Shopping Newsletter**) keeps readers up to date on competitions, exclusive shopping deals and special offers sending out all the latest news and tips, straight to their mailbox, every fortnight. 2020shops has a similar deal, as do a number of others but before you sign up with just any newsletter first make sure that a) there is also a simple way of unsubscribing in case you tire of it, and b) that the site will not pass your details on to a marketing company.

Shop

Shopping Newsletter

1 Introduction

Where there is a price comparison engine that covers the category of product you're after then that will undoubtedly point you to some of the specialist sites that will almost always offer better prices than general department stores. That said, the department stores or online malls have the advantage of bringing together a wide range of different lines under one virtual roof, and often simplify the whole buying process by having a single shopping basket and check out. Or if price is important you can always browse the department stores for ideas then hit the price comparison sites to try and get the best deal.

Among the things to remember when buying clothes or beauty products is that this really is time to check their returns policy, since if something turns up and you really don't like it then you don't want to have to pay the postage to send it back. So as to encourage shoppers many online stores have a no-quibble approach to returns so you don't have to worry, but they're not obliged to do so by law so it's wise to check their online policies. If they don't display a returns policy online then it's best to take your custom elsewhere. Again, because competition is fierce, most of the better sites have gone out of their way to make returns easy, so at the likes of Marks & Spencer you have a choice of having returns picked up by a courier or just dropping them off at your local shop.

For some reason clothes shopping is an area where there are also a few eye-catching shopper pleasers. Some sites, notably the ill-fated Boo.com, have tried to create 3D models that you can dress in order to see your clothes. Be careful about sizes as not only can a 'medium' vary hugely from one supplier to another but there is the potential confusion of UK, European, or American sizing appearing on the same site because the designers weren't sure what country you would be visiting it from – all the more reason to make entirely sure of the returns policy before you buy.

In terms of new thinking, one site – Lands' End – has brought in the idea of a shared shopping basket so you don't have to shop alone. The idea is that you can invite someone else online, perhaps a friend or relative, to join you in the online shop with both of you filling up just one basket. Whoever started the session must check out with the basket so you are by definition either invited or inviting someone else. It would certainly be a more intimate way of sharing a present with someone far away and provides a much more personal alternative to the ubiquitous shopping voucher as a present.

2020shops
www.2020shops.co.uk
Price comparison (supplied by DealTime), shopping tips and a forum where you can chime in about being a happy or an unhappy shopper.

Shopping Unlimited
www.shoppingunlimited.co.uk
Part of the *Guardian* newspaper's new media empire and so has a distinctly newspaper like feel to it but includes a number of reports, articles providing advice, and news about shopping online.

Littlewoods
www.littlewoods.co.uk
Littlewoods is now offering some 40,000 different products from its home shopping catalogue online, as well as store locators and the ability to manage your store account on the Web.

Marks & Spencer
www.marksandspencer.com
Flowers, womenswear, mens clothes, and home goods, though not the food range are all on offer with a 72-hour delivery service. Includes an 'as seen on

TV' section so if you saw it and liked it on the advert you can jump straight to the item to buy it.

John Lewis
www.johnlewis.com
Never knowingly undersold and a treasurehouse of quality gift ideas, sometimes with a classy hint of nostalgia about them (see toys). Clothes, furnishings, electronics, sports, it's all there.

Figleaves
www.figleaves.com
Figleaves are actually about the only item of underwear that this eye-poppingly huge range doesn't include. Lingerie, boxers, and T-shirts of all hues, including celebrity ranges like Elle Macpherson's and all the big name designers.

Boots
www.wellbeing.com
Don't be confused by the domain name, Wellbeing.com is indeed the familiar

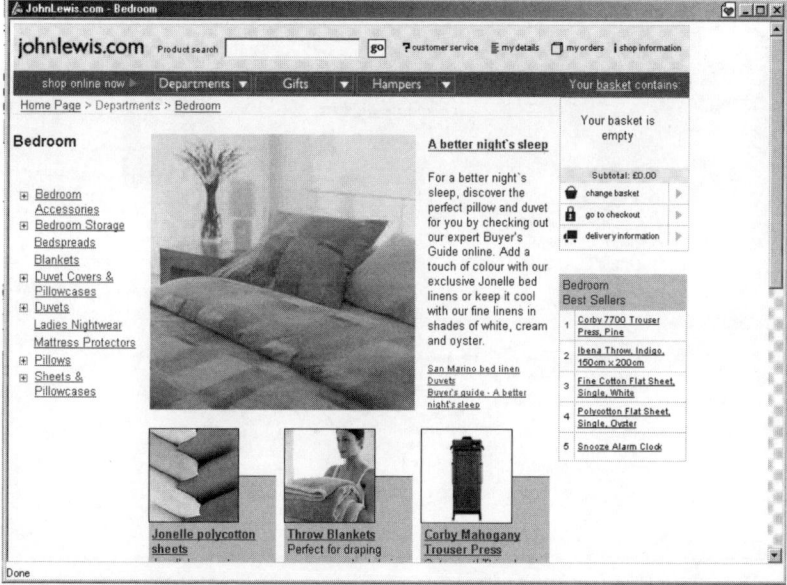

Fig.7.1 Never knowingly undersold and tough to beat on choice or quality.

Fig. 7.2   Actually figleaves are about the only undergarment not on offer on this site.

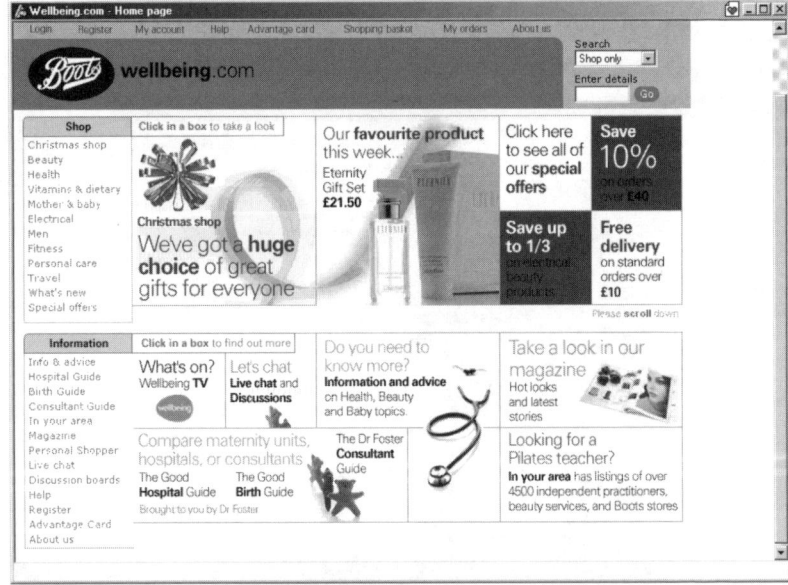

Fig. 7.3   Wellbeing.com, the healthcare site courtesy of the famous chemist also gives advice on wellbeing and even where to find Pilates instruction.

high street chemists with all the products you'd hope for plus a wealth of useful advice ranging from pregnancy guides to finding your nearest Pilates teacher.

Debenhams
www.debenhams.co.uk
Not one of the first to get online but with a site currently being revamped so hopefully soon to offer an even broader range.

Argos
www.argos.co.uk
The Argos approach to warehouse shops translates very well indeed to the Web with the benefit of a full stock range at your disposal.

Barclaysquare/Shopsmart
www.shopsmart.co.uk
Barclay Square was one of the first malls to be launched in the UK and the years have seen it now rolled into a new, and impressively broad ranged project called Shopsmart with good special offers and plenty of information.

E Directory
www.edirectory.co.uk
Vast. Huge number of shops crammed under one single URL and just gagging to sell you anything from Man U strips to flowers.

Kays
www.kaysnet.com
Catalogue shopping transported to the Web.

Next
www.next.co.uk
Another online catalogue specialist.

Lands' End
www.landsend.co.uk
Catalogue with nifty section on clearance sales.

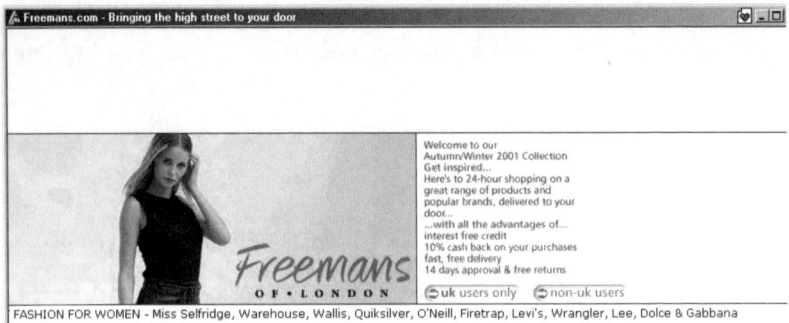

FASHION FOR WOMEN - Miss Selfridge, Warehouse, Wallis, Quiksilver, O'Neill, Firetrap, Levi's, Wrangler, Lee, Dolce & Gabbana

Fig. 7.4 Catalogue shopping becomes even more convenient when you can just click on what takes your fancy to buy it.

Freemans

www.freemans.com

'Bringing the high street to your door' – with a free returns policy and without the traffic wardens.

QVC

www.qvc.co.uk

Another home shopping specialist takes to cyberspace.

Kids' clothes

Kids Window

www.kidswindow.co.uk

Makes a change from Mothercare and lets you type in your child's age and sex to see a decent selection of kids' clothes.

Babycrest

www.babycrest.com

Newborns clothed here – very good gift box approach so you can get presents for friends' offspring without dragging yourself down the high street to do so.

National Schoolwear Centres

www.n-sc.co.uk

If the name sounds institutional it's perhaps not an accident since this is the place for uniforms – school, Cubs, sports, etc.

Walcot Woollies
www.walcotwoollies.co.uk
Hand-made designer knitwear.

Smellies

Fragrance Direct
www.fragrancedirect.co.uk
Useful Scent Searcher engine, wide range of brands, and cheap delivery help make this site worth the visit.

Boots
www.wellbeing.com
Familiar household name comes up trumps with this comprehensive site including all the big brands at down-to-earth prices.

Pharmacy 2 U
www.pharmacy2u.co.uk
Cheap and cheerful chemists with everything from Clarins skin care products to kids shampoo.

Garden
www.garden.co.uk
UK's largest pharmacy and perfumery, apparently.

Designer Discount
www.designerdiscount.co.uk
On the one hand people buy Yves St Laurent, Moschino, Paul Smith *et al* because they are perceived as being exclusive, on the other they want them at the same price as the high street cheapies. Best thing to do is to go to the site, check out their Dolce e Gabanna discounts, profit from the free UK delivery, and tell not a soul.

Sport and fitness

Sportsmart

www.sportsmart.co.uk

Most of the big brand names from sport plus some fitness advice and an order tracking service so you can find out why your Adidas kit hasn't shown up on time for Saturday's match.

Sweatband

www.sweatband.com

Vile name, great shop for sports kit for all of the more common sports (forget about it if you're into triathlon or Judo for example).

Extreme Pie

www.extremepie.com

Daft name, great shop for boarding (surf or snow), BMXing or just generally hanging around looking like Ali G.

Massive Arms

www.massivearms.com

No really, I didn't make this up. Absurd name, absurd idea, but there you go – the site sells a book aimed at those worried about having sand kicked in their faces by beach hunks.

Newitts

www.newitts.com

Newitts claims to be the largest mail-order supplier of sports equipment in the UK which presumably makes me the only person never to have heard of them.

Proline Sports

www.proline-sports.co.uk

For when it all goes wrong. Knee supports, kidney belts, and injury equipment generally.

Umbro Store
www.umbro.com
For official sports strips of most of Europe's top teams – and an arm and a leg if you have a family of teenagers demanding this year's strip (home AND away please).

CHAPTER

8

Domestic Bliss – Buying a Home, Furnishing a Home, Classifieds and Groceries

Property

If you're tired of the four walls you're looking at now going online can help you find a new place to call home. Sites such as Fish4 (www.fish4.co.uk) have over a quarter of a million homes on their books, go to AOL Keyword: **Property** and there is a finder to help you research your dream home. Or get advice on how to value the one you're already in – including tips for getting the best value on your home, and links out to sites that give you a feeling for relative prices in different areas, such as Up My Street (www.upmystreet.co.uk). You can also find out what your property is likely to be worth in the future thanks to the AOL House Price Predictor (for more turn to **Chapter 5, Finance**). Or perhaps you like the sound of a place, or recognise the postcode, but you're not sure where it is? Try a zoomable street map such as www.streetmap.co.uk which also gives you the option of an aerial view of your own area or the one that you're thinking of moving to. Up My Street (AOL Keyword: **UMS**) is a great way of learning a little more about an area – from sports and school facilities to the contact details of your local MP.

UMS

AOL's House and Home section has advice on looking for, finding, funding, surveying, and buying property. Choosing an estate agent and getting the most from them (hard to believe I know), tricks of the trade, finding surveyors in your area, gazumping the gazumpers, and even great building disasters (you may want to read this while hiding behind the sofa and peeking through your fingers); they're all there. From the flippant, but sadly oh-so-true advice of 'let's talk builder', to more practical tricks like surveying with a screwdriver or even Feng Shui'ing your home you can get all the advice online without being afraid of sounding like a muppet just because you had to ask. If you're put off by snooty estate agents or confused about the legal process then this is a great place to start getting your thoughts lined up and your finances sorted.

Fittings and furnishings, buying and DIY

Once you've got your dream home the chances are you're going to want to modify it. DIY is a national obsession – you only have to take a look at the TV schedules (AOL Keyword: **TV**) to see that if we're not baking or trimming our borders, we're making bookshelves (or bodging of course). For that, AOL has teamed up with B&Q (AOL Keyword: **DIY** or www.diy.com on the Web) to provide answers to everything from installing a new toilet to choosing paint or fitting a new door handle. If you don't find what you want explained then you can fire off your question by email and the answer joins a list of similar queries from other flummoxed folk. Dedicated calculators not only make light work of converting imperial to metric but also of such age-old headscratchers as calculating the amount of wallpaper or number of kitchen tiles you'll need to buy in order to avoid a second trip to the DIY superstore.

TV

DIY

Alternatively, you may either have too much sense or too little time to worry about DIY and prefer simply to buy your interior outright. No problem, there is no end of furnishings shops, and you can even size up furniture prices at comparison engines such as DealTime (www.espotting.dealtime.co.uk). Here are a few suggestions to get you going.

BBC Good Homes
www.goodhomes.beeb.com
The BBC is a non commercial organisation but its commercial arm, the Beeb, is more than happy to turn a penny and give you guidance on what to go for in the process.

B&Q
www.diy.com
Whether you're after power tools or plumbing, doors or decking you'll find it at DIY along with the advice on projects that makes this much more than a simple shop site. Nor does that advice just mean a few quick tips, in some cases, such as the kitchen planner, there are entire downloadable guides to help you with your home improvement.

Fig. 8.1 The best prices, and advice, for home improvement.

Fig. 8.2   B & Q doesn't just sell DIY material, it also provides really useful guides to improvements you can make.

Comet

www.comet.co.uk

Comet's range of electrical goods extends to vacuum cleaners, cooling systems and heaters for the home as well a full range of white goods from washing machines to dishwashers.

McCord

www.emccord.co.uk

Interior designer McCord features hand-picked designer products for home, garden, and office selected from around the world. Whether it's storage, lighting, or furnishings that interest you you'll find inspiration, on this site.

Bed Bath & Home

www.bedbathandhome.co.uk

'The most fun way to furnish your home on the net' includes some great nursery themes (Harry Potter, Thomas the Tank engine, etc.) to help make bedtime fun, as well as towels, bathrobes, curtains, and fabrics for the bathroom and indeed the rest of the home.

Fig. 8.3 All your home electrics and electronics in one place.

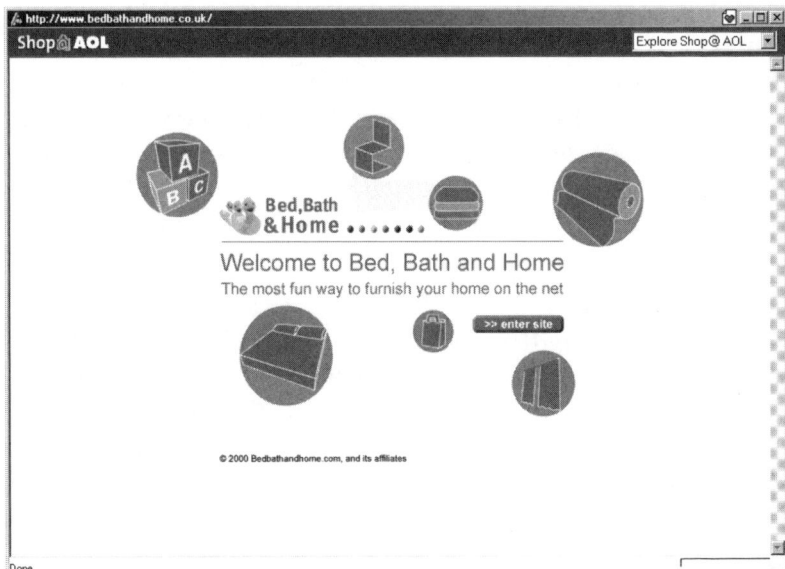

Fig. 8.4 'The most fun way to furnish your home' and first stop for those Winnie the Pooh bedcovers.

World Gallery

www.worldgallery.co.uk

Prints, reproductions, frames, and special limited edition prints for tastes that span the spectrum from Michaelangelo to Rothko.

Easy Art

www.easyart.co.uk

Prints, etchings, photographs, and the golden age of posters, but also interactive fun, art for the kids, and competitions.

Crocus

www.crocus.co.uk

'Gardeners by nature' with cut flowers, plants, seeds, bulbs, tips and plant finders to help you pick the best vegetation for your garden.

Vintage Yard Furniture

www.vintageyard.com

Because the fact that you use the Web doesn't mean you don't appreciate times gone by.

Pinehouse.co.uk

www.pinehouse.co.uk

Not just pine but 2000 different items of wood furniture, mainly pine or oak.

BrandFind

www.brandfind.co.uk

Fast way to get what you want from the online furniture shops.

Your Price Furniture

www.yourpricefurniture.co.uk

Beds, bedrooms, home offices etc. with free delivery to the United Kingdom. Products include beds, kids beds, bedrooms, home office, etc.

Peter Hall & Son Furniture Workshop

www.peter-hall.co.uk
Includes restoration work as well as new products.

Pineology

www.pineology.co.uk
An ology is it now? Beds, chests, chairs, and cabinets from Chester.

Pine Online

www.pineonline.co.uk
We just don't seem to be able to get enough of this pine stuff.

Beds 999

www.beds999.co.uk
Where they sell, erm, beds.

Nearly new

Classifieds

Buying new is fine, but the Net is also there for those of us looking for second hand bargains too, and in particular you may never need to buy a paper again in order to thumb through the classifieds. The nice thing about classified ads online is that instead of waiting all week for the edition that has what you want, then poring through page after page of ads you can simply go online and type in what you're looking after, or what you want to pay, or even your postcode and be told where the nearest one is. AOL Keyword: **Classifieds** lets you specify where you are and what you want, and it does the rest. Of course you may not be bothered about distance – people tend to be more prepared to travel to buy a car than they are to buy a microwave – in which case you simply type in as much or as little detail as you need to find the thing you're looking for. An asparagus steamer in SE1? A dishwasher in W11? No problem. Out on the Web the same approach will find you whatever your house needs simply by checking out the likes of PreLoved (www.preloved.co.uk), or Net Trader (www.nettrader.co.uk/). From sofas in Sussex to toasters in Telford, it's all there.

Classifieds

Food and drink

Buying food and drink isn't so much a question of saving money, more of saving time. Instead of finding a parking spot (or dodging wardens), avoiding other people's kids, and hauling all your goodies back home, simply click your way through the week's grocery shopping and relax: your produce will be delivered to your door (or your office if you prefer).

AOL offers Tesco's own delivery service (www.tesco.com) which costs a flat £5 fee, no matter how many weeks worth of shopping, or hundred-weight of beer cans you happen to be ordering. Asda also delivers to many areas (www.asda.com), as does Waitrose (www.waitrose.com) and Sainsbury (www.sainsburystoyou.co.uk). Alternatively you'll find pretty much all of these and many others by using AOL Keywords: **Food** or **Shopping**.

Food

Shopping

For anyone curious about organic food, or squeamish at the thought of fish genes in their tomatoes and poisons on their pears there is also a lot of information available from the Organics section of AOL. Once you've learnt everything you ever wanted to know about modern food production you may then opt to go for curiously wrinkly, but wholly healthy fruit and veg only to then find you don't seem to have a supplier in your area. Once again online is to the rescue for the far-flung and the time-poor. Try deliveries from the supermarkets named above, or the Organic Delivery Company (www.organicdelivery.co.uk), or Absolute Organic (www.absolutorganic.co.uk).

Wine Shop

Similarly, for the thirsty yet lazy, AOL Keyword: **Wine Shop** should offer you everything you need to wet your whistle in style, or you can go on the Web to find the same selection courtesy of WineSmart (www.winesmart.com), Chateau Online (www.chateauonline.co.uk) or Virgin Wines (www.virginwines.com). So why would you buy wine online? Well for a start the prices are going to beat everything but the dodgy geezers in white vans. In addition, all of the services listed here (and everything on offer in Shop@AOL) offer price and satisfaction guarantees, plus there's a wealth of information you're simply not going to get from peering at labels. Finally there are no assistants there to give you funny looks just because you don't know your Neuchatel from your Nottage Hill. You don't even need to know what you want or what questions to ask because online there are automatic tools to help you. Take the Virgin wine wizard for example. A series of questions about what you usually spend and why, followed by a 'taste test' to see what type of wines you tend to go for leads to a series of suggestions. If you buy a recommended wine and don't like it you get your money back. Sorted.

Asda
www.asda.com

Waitrose
www.waitrose.com

Sainsbury
www.sainsburystoyou.co.uk

Tesco
www.tesco.co.uk

Organic Delivery Company
www.organicdelivery.co.uk

Absolute Organic
www.absolutorganic.co.uk

WineSmart
www.winesmart.com

Fig. 8.5 Shop without leaving your desk and have your groceries delivered for when you get home.

Chateau Online

www.chateauonline.co.uk

Virgin Wines

www.virginwines.com

Berry Bros & Rudd

www.bbr.com

Fine wines to discerning customers for 300 years.

Wine Online

www.wineonline.co.uk

Wines to buy and tasting notes to help you choose.

Whittard of Chelsea

www.whittard.com

Well you'll be needing tea and coffees for the morning after.

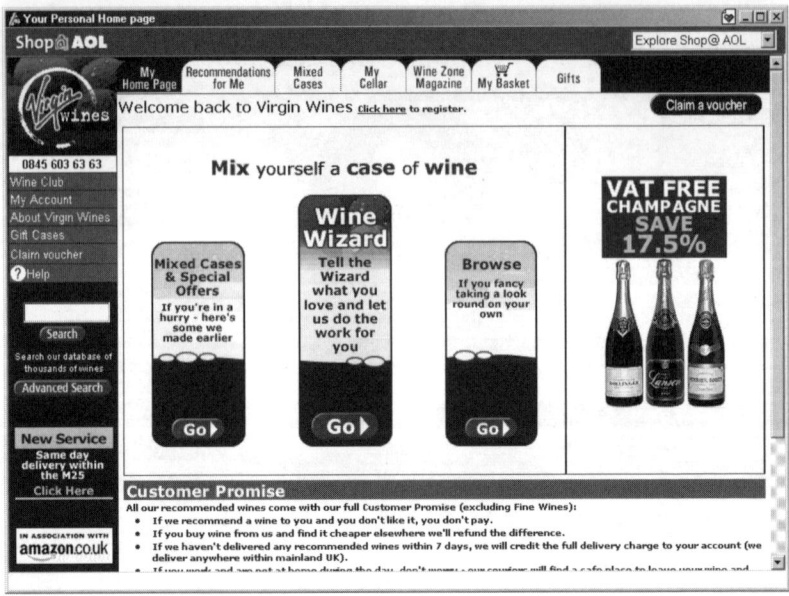

Fig. 8.6 Not only will it help you choose wine, but you don't have to pay if you don't like it.

CHAPTER

9

Transport – Wheels, Wings and Water

Buying cars

Whenever the slogan 'rip-off Britain' is bandied around you can be pretty sure that someone is going to mention car prices as it became increasingly clear throughout the nineties that we were paying more for new cars than the rest of Europe. The Web has changed that forever. Instant comparisons and access to information have turned the tables on the traditional relationship between buyer and seller. Time was when a car buyer would turn up at a showroom to be fleeced by a sympathetic sounding man who would grudgingly throw in a radio as an extra in return for an asking price several thousand higher than that paid by the car buyer's continental counterparts. In the US, Priceline (www.priceline.co.uk, the company that introduced name-your-own-price air travel (see **Chapter 5**) shook the car industry to its roots by doing the same with cars. Because would-be owners were able to propose a price to every dealer in the country the nation itself soon came to a new, brokered under-standing about just what a particular car model was worth – and it wasn't the list price in the showroom. In the UK the fact that you can instantly check the cost of that model in neighbouring countries, complete with the cost of conversion to right hand drive, meant that we can now see exactly what a car should cost. Dealers once tried to discourage customers buying from overseas, even if overseas meant Northern Ireland, but EU regulations insisting on an open marketplace mean that all is now fair in cross-border bargain hunting for cars.

5 Finance

Motoring

Go to AOL Keyword: **Motoring** and you'll find a New and Used car search on the main page, plus Buyer's Guides, Insurance and more. On the Web there's simply no end of advice on car buying, some of the best can be found at Motoring Which? or at Parker's Online (www.parkers.co.uk) or Autohit (www.autohit.com), which not only give advice on specific models, new or used, but also help step you through the decision-making process of exactly which wheels were made for you. There's also the crash test safety information available from the AA – remember how about once a year there's an announcement on the news about which models have failed it? Well now's the time to refresh your memory and make sure you're not about to buy something that crumples like a Coke can by checking out www.theaa.co.uk/motoringandtravel/safety.

Once you've seen the prices being offered online you will wonder how the UK ever fell for the exorbitant prices of yesteryear.

Exchange & Mart
www.exchangeandmart.co.uk
A decidedly groovy-looking interface makes the online version of this venerable ads paper a colourful great. Thousands of new and used cars for sale.

Autotrader
www.autotrader.co.uk
New cars, used cars, finding a dealer in your area – a simple search will reveal all at Exchange & Mart's big rival.

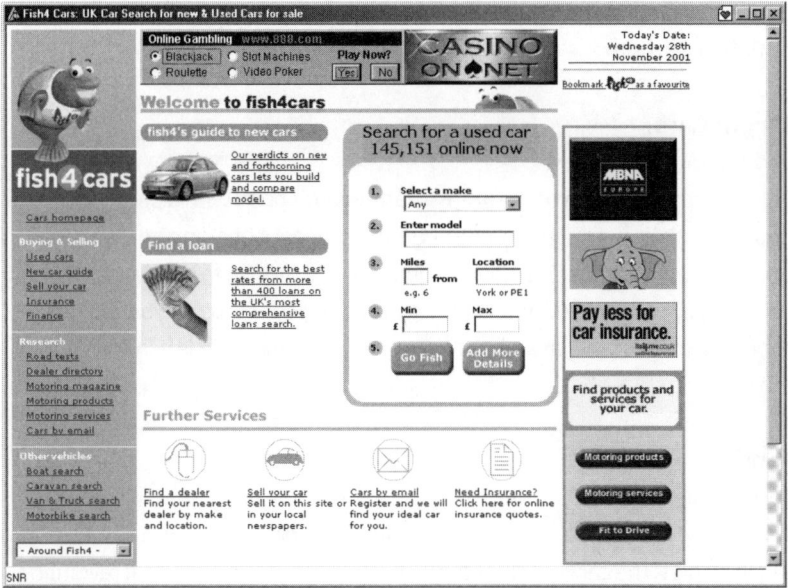

Fig. 9.1 If it's a motor you're after, the Web will find it for you faster.

Fish4cars

www.fish4cars.co.uk

Another collection of small ads mainly to help in the search for second hand cars.

New cars

Carbusters

www.carbusters.com

Sounds like some kind of hard-talking car crimebusting unit and for the motor trade it might as well be. Carbusters is the motorised arm of the Consumer Association and was instrumental in forcing prices down and ending the rip-off Britain era.

OneSwoop

www.oneswoop.com

European imports without the hassle of sorting out anything yourself – except how much you want to save. Standard savings over UK costs are from two to three thousand pounds per car, which is great news, unless you've recently bought a car from the showroom.

Virgin Cars

www.virgincars.com

The motorised division of the Branson army is equipped with a particularly fine 'wizard' or helper to step you through the process of finding your dream car and saving thousands. Site comes complete with advice from Quentin Wilson (from Top Gear), and even if Quentin's toothy gleam follows you around the room his image is the last relic of the showroom smoothie left in the car buying process.

Jamjar

www.jamjar.com

Amusingly enough for a company with the logo of a little red phone on wheels, this is the car branch of the Direct Insurance company that revolutionised insurance sales by taking out the middleman. Jamjar aims to do simply the same for buying a motor. Predictably it also takes the opportunity of offering the financing to help you buy a new car and, yup, it will sell you the insurance for it too.

Motorbikes

Bikes on the Web haven't taken off with quite the enthusiasm that cars have, which could be down to the fact that bikers have long been aware of the possibility of saving money by buying foreign bikes on the 'grey import' market. It's a great deal easier chasing down a bike deal abroad not least since there is no steering wheel to move to the other side. Nonetheless the Web remains the fastest way of tracking down prices on the fastest two wheelers.

Bike Trader

www.biketrader.co.uk

Bike Trader is the motorbike section of Auto Trader (other sections include caravans and boats).

Cambridge Lambretta
www.lambretta.co.uk
Not just Lambrettas as it happens but a range of classic Italian scooters with old and new models on offer as well as servicing and spares – 'from a rivet to a restoration' as the site puts it.

Scooter Zone
www.scooterzone.co.uk
A messy looking and needlessly animated site in its current incarnation, Scooter Zone nonetheless provides the UK with a 24-hour virtual showroom for when you just have to decide what to buy at 3a.m.

Carnell
www.carnell-bikes.co.uk
If you're unfamiliar with the Carnell brand you'll probably know it better as Motorcycle City, and as Europe's largest dealership it offers up to 30% off new bikes.

Boats

Boats for Sale
www.boatsforsale.co.uk
From jet skis to canal boats and rubber inflatables, not to be confused with:

Boats for Sale – Boat Trader
www.boats-for-sale.com
This site has thousands of boats and, rather usefully, can be searched by price as well as specification.

Aeroplanes

As you may have gathered, you can buy pretty much anything online …

UK Planes for sale
www.planes4saleonline.com
Used planes in the UK.

Aeromart

www.aeromart.co.uk
New or used, UK-based or abroad, if it has wings or rotors you'll find it here.

Submarines

See, you really can buy pretty much anything!

Project Boats

www.projectboats.com/submarines.html
Used subs for sale.

Russian Nuclear Submarine Juliette

www.subexpo.com
Just as it sounds, a Russian submarine originally intended as a platform for intercontinental ballistic missiles. Oddly enough this sub was actually put on auction on eBay at one point, which goes to show you what a wild world online auctioning is.

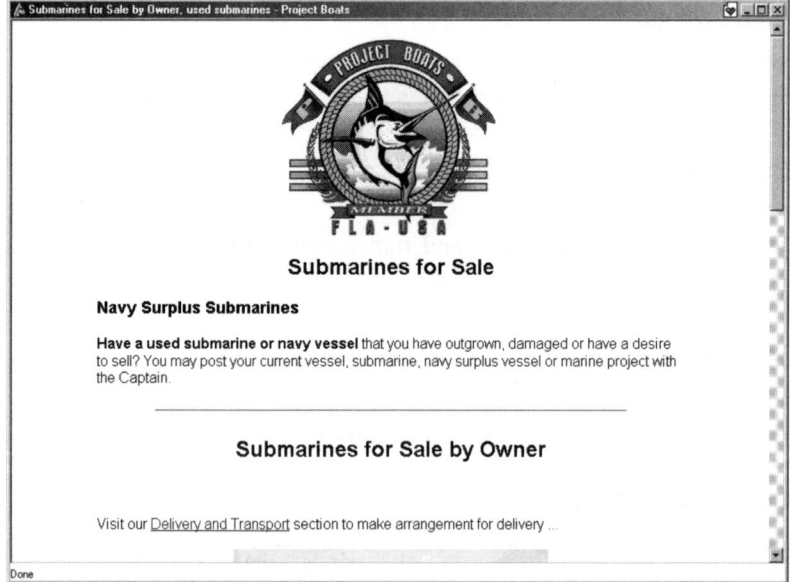

Fig. 9.2   Yes, you can buy pretty much anything online.

CHAPTER

10

Auctions

I think my first understanding of an auction came from reading the adventures of Paddington Bear in which our loveable cuddly beastie found himself the unwitting owner of an object because he made the mistake of waving and thus encouraging bidding. Ever since, the TV, stage, and big screen have all reinforced that image. Auctions, the message is clear, may have great bargains, but they're fraught with danger and one twitch of the nose could buy something costing millions.

On the Net, you can set aside any ideas about tense scenes with hostile counter bidders, or prices in guineas, or gavels, or a sneeze costing you millions. Online auctions just don't work like that. Someone offers up an item, and people take turns to bid over periods that can stretch over days. Yes, there are some really great prices to be had (how about three days' hotel accommodation for a fiver? Or a foreign city break for just over a tenner?), but aside from bargain hunting the real appeal for most auction fans is that there are some really oddball items up for grabs. Looking for a Captain Scarlet ray gun? How about an Airfix kit that's been out of production since you were a kid? An Edwardian otter's paw brooch? Or a FireWire cable for a digital camera? Where

Fig. 10.1 AOL brings you the very best of online auctions – unbelievable prices, sometimes for unbelievable items.

else are you going to find all of the above on a single site? Auctions are a wonderland of things you never knew you needed, as well as a source of knock-down pricing on objects you knew you did. In the past that appeal has also brought the wrong kind of attention as people have tried to use them as a means of fencing stolen goods. The French government has even taken action against one auction site because it was offering Nazi memorabilia (banned in France). Some of the bad publicity is merited but on the whole the reputable sites are working hard to clean up their act. There are certain key differences that make an online auction very different from an online shop though, so it's as well to understand how it works, what the risks are to you, and how to shop safely.

The first thing to understand is that there is more than one type of auction site. Some of them are simply the online sites of well-established traditional auctioneers from the world of guineas and gavels. Often the site is merely a shop window to an auction that will be taking place in the wood panelled rooms of their London office. In that case the auction site may actually be no more than a catalogue of the goods going under the hammer. In others it is a means of offering a bid – like a sealed bid left in an envelope with an auctioneer. For such sites the rules are exactly the same as leaving a sealed bid with a traditional auction house, except that you will probably be asked to register to establish who you are. But when most people talk about online auctions they don't really mean Sotheby's or Bonham's, they mean the likes of QXL and eBay.

QXL, eBay, and others such as Yahoo! auctions are often person-to-person auctions where someone in Bournemouth offers up their goodies for sale and you all get to bid for them. In a person-to-person exchange, the auction site is not usually responsible for the transaction. Instead you are, and on an 'as seen' basis so 'buyer beware' is a useful motto. You are reliant on the seller sending it to you, so if they say it must have got lost in the post you have no company to turn to. Of course auction companies do all they can to ensure that everyone is happy – for example many of them feature ratings that allow previous customers to say whether a seller is trustworthy and whether the goods were described accurately. Which is great if the thing you want comes from a regular at the auction, but not if it's a one-off from someone clearing out the garage. Chances are you aren't completely in the cold if it all goes wrong, but the savvy shopper will once again do his or her homework.

First check out the auction site and its schemes. Some of them carry insurance that means they will pick up some or all of the loss if you get ripped off. Make sure there isn't any small print that excludes your particular deal; like the insistence that the seller must have a positive feedback rating, for example. Researching the seller is a great idea where possible, and with services such as eBay you will find a list of previous sales made and who bought them complete with comments. On the other hand such systems are not foolproof and you should use a little healthy cynicism when checking out rating systems for sellers. Ratings that go back a long way and offer glowing testimonials usually mean you're on safe ground, but it is relatively easy to fox the system and have yourself rated really highly in the short term. If you can pay by credit card then you're covered by the credit card guarantees (see **Chapter 1**). Not all private sellers are going to take cards though, so you may be asked to pay by cheque. Ensuring that you can cancel the cheque if the goods don't arrive in time is one way of protecting yourself, using an escrow service is a better one. Escrow services basically mean that the money isn't paid straight to the seller, but is instead handed to a trusted third party so that the seller doesn't get the dosh until the buyer has received the goods. Escrow services such as I-Escrow (www.iescrow.com) usually charge a fee for this service but it can be as little as a couple of quid which you may get the seller to split with you. Never pay cash.

1 Introduction

Once you have bought an item it may be a good idea to get in touch with the seller and arrange for a recorded delivery rather than just using the post. You will probably have to pay the extra but it does take away the doubt about when something will arrive and it removes any 'lost in the post' arguments.

How do I go about bidding?

Warnings over, now it's time to shop. The first step is to register because while anyone can browse, only registered users can **buy** and **sell** on an auction service like eBay. Registration is free, and no more complex than the million other things you sign up for online. Once registered you get a user ID and a password, and you're ready to buy and sell. Next up you find what you want, either by putting in a search word, by looking items up category by category, or best of all by giving up any idea of working that morning and instead surfing aimlessly through all the stuff that's for sale. Some sites like eBay let you search specifically for items that are based in the UK. There's nothing to stop you buying from the US, but you need to be aware of where the seller is or else you're going to have a shock when it comes to paying for shipping (which is your problem, remember). The auction site may also have a page you can personalise (like 'My eBay', or 'My QXL') which allows you to specify your particular fascination for Brian Eno vinyl, first edition children's books, or whatever. The site will then offer up tips and advice on buying for that category and provides a one-stop shop to track all of the things that you are trying to buy.

Once you've found what you want, take a look at the minimum bid price, and the bidding increment (the amount it goes up by every time you take the price to the next level), decide what you want to spend, and bid. Could be that's all you need to do if the item is not in great demand, but the chances are this is just the beginning. In some auctions someone else now needs to come along and offer a higher price to get the bidding moving. You check back to see if you're still tops, and decide on whether or not to offer more if you find you're currently outbid. At the end of a given period of time (always clearly shown) the last and highest bid seals the deal.

Straightforward enough, but not actually the way that sites like eBay function. Instead many auction sites work on what's called proxy bidding which might seem more complex, but actually works to save money for bidders. The way it works is that you see something you like, and notice that the minimum reserve price (the least the seller will accept) is a tenner and that the bidding increments are a quid a shot. This particular obscure object of desire is whispering to you that you have to have it and in your heart of hearts you decide that you really couldn't or shouldn't go above £30 for it so you bid £30. Why not just bid £11? Because unless the item is really obscure, or only just been put on sale you'll probably find that someone else has already done that. What happens when you put in £30 is that the system doesn't show that sum, what it does is check to see if that sum is the highest bid, and if it is it shows that it is top bid, but only by bidding one increment (in this case a quid) over the previous top bid. So if someone else bids £14 for the object they're still outbid by you, but instead of ploughing in and blowing the whole £30 what the auction software does is beat their bid on your behalf so you automatically offer £15. If a bidding war starts then the price will rise to £30 (and higher if you want to go for it) but if it doesn't reach that amount you will only pay one pound more than the second highest offer. What it does mean, however, is that while you know who is leading the bidding you don't really know how much they're prepared to go up to which can mean that a price stays the same for days, then in the closing minutes of an auction it will shoot up as a proxy bid matches all comers. Which is how an object seemingly on sale for ages at £5 can suddenly shoot up to £500 because one canny (or simply besotted) customer had actually set a personal top whack of that much and a latecomer forced the bidding up skywards. All of which usually means that an auction is a slow, nervy event with no one blinking until the last day or even the last few minutes at which it can erupt into a frenzy of chaotic (and costly) activity. Which is the whole fun of the thing.

Incidentally, some sites will let you know if your bid is beaten by email. Some don't but that's often not so much of a problem as it sounds because the chances are that as you get to the end of the auction period you will be online staring at the screen, biting your nails, and seeing if you get the item. If you forgot that you bid for something are you sure you really wanted it?

Auction Guide

www.auctionguide.com

Not an auction site *per se* but an information and search engine that helps you find what you want from auction sites all over the globe.

Auction Watch

www.auctionwatch.com

Search dozens of auction sites at once to find that elusive item to bid for.

eBay UK

www.ebay.co.uk

There's a lot of local UK stuff for sale, but it also links directly into the parent site so you often find yourself looking at goodies that are currently on the other side of the pond – which could be either a good thing, or a bad thing, depending on what you're looking for.

QXL

www.qxl.com

Home grown auction site, which is reflected in the kind of things on sale. Well established and good reputation, deals in a broad spread of goods from tasteful to tat.

Yahoo! Auctions

www.auctions.yahoo.co.uk

The portal site cashes in on the large amount of through traffic on its pages to promote its own auction site.

Sothebys

www.sothebys.com

Gateway to Sotheby's auctions but with the added interest of online-only stuff, although this is still more along the 'ancient and ethnographic art' lines than the 'gubbins from my garage' approach.

Bonham's

www.bonhams.com

Like the above, a well established auction house providing a window on the Web into its forthcoming auctions.

iCollector

www.icollector.com

Online auctioneer but a class above the usual old toys and second hand electricals brigade. Worth a look for art works and old wine amongst other things.

Aucland

www.aucland.co.uk

Fair scope from rarity to rubbish.

Business-auctions.com

www.business-auctions.com

Clouds, silver linings, and bargains as businesses that go bust auction off their office equipment.

Holiday Auctions

www.holiday-auctions.co.uk

Just what it sounds like, but not necessarily cheaper than the bucket shops or wonders like Priceline. If it's travel you're after then best take a look at *Chapter 9*.

9 Transport – Wheels, Wings and Water

APPENDIX

Your Rights, Their Wrongs

Know your rights

Before dishing out the dosh it pays to know where you stand with the law. The bottom line is that the UK doesn't exclude online shopping from any of the consumer's statutory rights so everything that applies to faulty goods or services in a real shop applies just as forcibly in its virtual counterpart. In fact the online shopper actually gets extra protection on top of the existing rights, thanks to the Distance Selling Regulations which came into force on 31 October 2000. The Distance Selling Regulations apply to online shopping, catalogue purchasing by post, interactive TV shopping, or shopping channels on TV where you respond by buying over the phone. Anything in fact where the person you are buying from is not actually standing in front of you in a shop.

Under your normal statutory rights the products you buy should fit their description and be fit for their purpose. Basically it has to do what it says on the box or you get your money back. If goods don't turn out to be what they were advertised to be or are in any way faulty then you should get in touch with the supplier immediately. Unless you're in the habit of bugging your own phone it's a good idea to make sure that anything you point out on the blower is also set down in writing and make sure you keep notes of all contact and correspondence.

English law is pretty clear on the matter of faulty products – if it doesn't work it has to go back. That doesn't stop suppliers from clouding the issue, however, or even honestly getting it wrong (well it could happen). No matter what some suppliers would have you believe it is not the case that you sign away your right to reject a product as faulty just because you had to sign to receive the goods. Almost all deliveries involve signing for the goods, that doesn't mean they have the right to be faulty. It's also worth noting that if the seller offers to put the problem right that doesn't affect your statutory rights either. If the 'repaired' product still doesn't do what it says on the box then you still have the right to reject the goods. It is also the supplier's responsibility to pay for the return of goods if they're faulty, so you shouldn't be charged for returning faulty goods if they're faulty, even if a repair has already been attempted.

To the above rights the new Regulations add a few specific notes for the online buyer. Online shoppers have the right to clear, written information before they place the order, and a 'cooling off' period during which the order can be cancelled without any reason being given, for which the supplier has to make a full refund. The idea is that it's easy to get carried away and go click happy when online shopping, not least since a lot of the standard tricks of the trade, like one-click ordering and even the humble virtual shopping basket, are all geared towards getting you to commit to buying more than you originally went to the shop for. In a real shop you usually have that moment in front of the till when the little voice inside you points out that you don't really need a dozen full-size bouncy castles. Online, however, where you can click to your heart's content, tap in a card number, and then forget about it you may only realise the full extent of your cyber-consumer madness when an articulated lorry full of bouncy castles arrives outside your door. Don't panic. The law now gives you seven working days as a cooling off period in which you can cancel that order and with it any credit agreement you may have entered into (bouncy castles don't come cheap you know). It's important to know that that a phone call cancelling an order is not enough – you have to inform Bouncy

Castles R-Us that you've come to your senses by a letter, a fax, or an email and you'd be very wise to keep a copy. If you paid in advance the law says you must have your pennies back in the piggy bank within thirty days. Be warned though that you may have to pay for the cost of returning goods, or of having them collected, and if that's the case it's well worth finding out what the company charges to collect, and comparing that to how cheaply you can get them despatched yourself.

The bad news is that some things aren't covered, usually for some pretty commonsense reasons. Food and drink for example – nope, it's no good ordering forty Hawaiian pizzas only to email seven working days later to say that the pineapple looks funny and you're not paying for them. Likewise other perishables like flowers are excluded, even if you did end up having a row or he/she stood you up. Nor does a product actually have to wilt, rot, or smell funny to count as perishable. Anything with a 'shelf life' like newspapers or magazines can claim to be excluded from the seven-day period. I haven't seen a test case but presumably if your kids' favourite footie team decides to come up with a new strip since you ordered, as they seem to do every couple of weeks, then the same perishable argument could apply. The obvious answer is to think before you buy anything that wouldn't be just as desirable a week later and of course remember the golden rule: don't shop drunk.

Excluding fresh goods from the cooling off period is just common sense, but there are some less obvious cases where the letter of the law doesn't fully protect you. By and large online shops don't actually penalise you for changing your mind, rather the opposite. There are even wine shops (see **Chapter 8**) which will waive payment if you decide you don't like the wine you ordered – even though you've already drunk the stuff. Such policies are made out of the goodness of their marketing strategies and aren't enshrined in the law. It may come as a surprise, for example, to find that those shrink-wrapped CDs, videos, or software packages are exempt from the cooling off period the minute you tear off the plastic. Which is not to say the shops won't take them back (see the following section on Many Happy Returns), just that they aren't legally obliged.

8 Food and drink

Tailor-made goods are exempt too, presumably because Pavarotti kept changing his mind about those made-to-measure lycra running shorts, and travel arrangements including package holidays that are sold for specific dates don't come with a cooling off period. Sadly, but understandably, betting, gaming and lottery services are specifically excluded too. Which is a crying shame – just how useful would it be to be allowed to call up a week after the Grand National and ask for your stake back because you'd changed your mind?

Don't forget that as reassuring as the UK Distance Selling Regulations may be, they don't apply to a shop based in another country, something you may well want to bear in mind before snapping up that amazing deal from overseas.

If you want any further details on your rights as a shopper, online or otherwise, there is a leaflet available from the Office of Fair Trading called 'Shopping from Home; the facts at your fingertips' which is available from www.oft.gov.uk/html/distance/index.htm. The Office of Fair Trading (www.oft.gov.uk) has also got together with the Department of Trade and Industry (www.dti.gov.uk) to produce a guide called 'Home shopping: your rights as a consumer' (http://www.ecdti.co.uk/CGIBIN/PERLCON.PL) which is available in over a dozen languages including Welsh, Arabic, Bengali, Cantonese, Gujarati, Hindi, Punjabi, Somali, Turkish, Urdu, and Vietnamese or as an audiotape for the visually impaired.

Delivering on promises

Buying the goods is one thing, getting your eager paws on them is another. Delivery is often one of the great sticking points of online shopping because after having been dazzled by the click speed with which you can shed your money, you then have to sit around while a box is taken out of a warehouse in Boston (Lincs. or Mass. – of which more in a minute), loaded into a very un-cyber grubby old lorry, driven through the less than cutting edge traffic jams of our roads, then delivered to the wrong address or while you're out so you have to collect it from a sorting office. The sheer speed of cyber shopping is one of the great appeals, so it's hardly surprising that the impatient often skim over the issue of delivery, and in particular of delivery cost. Even people who carefully shop around on the Web for the cheapest CDs and games can end up blowing all their savings, and then some, by not totting up the delivery charges. Nor is it just impatience that's to blame – delivery (shipping) costs are something many sites prefer to lose in the small print.

Delivery terms are meant to be clearly displayed and, since they are part of the cost, that is a legal requirement under the Distance Selling Regulations. There is no specific requirement about the means of delivery, however, and that's where there's so much margin for misunderstanding. The *Which?* Web Trader policy specifies that retailers displaying the Web Trader logo have to deliver within 30 days, unless the consumer has specifically agreed to a longer period. AOL's Shop@AOLPromise states that retailers must display details as to how delivery will physically take place and estimated date of delivery. Outside of such voluntary schemes the only legal requirement is that they stipulate the cost.

Shipping costs vary enormously, partly because different sites opt for different methods of delivery, partly because some sites choose to subsidise delivery while some sites seem to take a margin on it. Certainly it's hard to match up the different rates charged by shopping sites with the rates charged by the post office. Many sites offer the option of ordinary delivery (which can be either by first or second class post) or some kind of express service, often for the next day, which is rarely worth the extra unless you are very impatient or you really left it late for that all-important present. In the latter case the extra postage may well be a small price to pay for sparing your life.

In many cases, however, the difference between fast and slow delivery is minimal and paying more doesn't always guarantee better service.

A quick way of seeing the difference delivery makes to pricing is to use AOL's price comparison engine which doesn't just tot up the product cost but also compares delivery charges across different sites. AOL users can find it by typing in AOL Keyword: **Price Comparison**. If you are not an AOL user go to the address http://www.shop.aol.co.uk/pricecomparison/uk_pricecomparison.adp.

Price Comparison

Inputting a well-known DVD, for example, turns up the information that the cost of the disc varies (at time of writing) from £15.99 to £18.99 depending on the retailer. To this you have to add delivery, which is usually in the area of £1 to £1.50, though in one case it costs as much as £1.75 and in a couple of others is free. You might expect the most expensive discs to come with the cheapest delivery charge since the retailer has clearly covered that cost in their margins but you would be wrong. Bizarrely the retailer with the lowest asking price for the DVD also turns out to be one of those offering free delivery, meaning that when you've taken into account the delivery as well the cheapest disc works out as £15.99 as opposed to the most expensive at £20.73. The difference in promised delivery time for that, incidentally is that the expensive one (at nearly a third more in total) should be sent out in one day, the cheapest says one to two days. Not too hard to work out which one you'd go to there.

Checking for a single paperback book, the results show that the difference in delivery cost ranges from £2.95 to free. The £2.95 isn't even the fastest delivery service so it pays to take a look before you order. When buying a number of items at once – particularly books, which are often not available at the same time – look for the option to have them all sent to you in one package. Obviously this involves some commonsense since there may be one book that is waiting for a reprint next year, but if they are likely to come in drips and drabs over the course of a week or so it is well worth instructing the seller to wait until all the books are ready then send them at once. If you have them sent to you one at a time you may end up having the joy of what seems like Christmas every day but the postage prices will almost certainly wipe out any cost saving from buying online.

All of which is fairly straightforward when you're buying from a single shop like Amazon (www.amazon.co.uk) or Books Online (www.bol.co.uk) but less clear when you buy from an online mall which features a one 'shopping basket' system but includes many suppliers. Those suppliers may each have different delivery mechanisms and tariffs, so before agreeing to buy anything make sure you know exactly what you're going to pay to have it sent to you, and how long it will take to do so.

Many Happy Returns

Hopefully you'll never need to send anything back because everything will be just hunky dory, but in the event that you get sent the wrong thing, or it doesn't work (see **Know your rights** above), or you change your mind then you're going to find yourself in the world of the returns policy. Generally speaking this is not a problem zone, and if you're buying from sellers with the *Which?* Web Trader tick of approval or the Shop@AOL seal of confidence then you can relax in the knowledge that their returns policy is straightforward and accommodating. Sometimes, however, you will want to buy outside of such safe zones, and when you do make sure you've taken the moment or so it takes to look at the return policy. You might think that if you buy online from a well-known high street shop then you can return the goods or make and exchange just by walking into your branch. This is not always the case, since the online arms of some retailers are financially and logistically (you know, warehouses and lorries and stuff) separate from the bricks and mortar version. If there is no return policy information on the site then think seriously about buying elsewhere. If you buy from a seller outside the UK then returns could be very expensive and if you're sending something back because you changed your mind you may well have to pick up the cost of getting shot of them.

Who to turn to if it all goes wrong

If, heaven forbid, something doesn't turn out as it should then don't panic because you're not alone and the chances are that you're not about to lose your money. That said it's certainly not impossible that you may end up wrangling with a rogue trader about whether or not the goods or service were up to scratch. If the retailer is a site displaying the hallmark of a consumer protection service like *Which?* or AOL, then those bodies will act as arbitrators. In fact if you ever find yourself dissatisfied with a site and it has some kind of quality assurance logo then make sure you complain to that body because it helps them monitor consumer satisfaction. If *Which?* or AOL get involved the likelihood is that the site will see the error of its ways the moment the spectre of bad publicity rears its head. Most companies are proud to display a quality control mark and have worked hard to maintain it. Being stripped of it is the shopping site equivalent of having your epaulettes pulled off and your sword broken in front of everyone.

Not all sites are in such schemes, however, and in some cases you may not even be sure if you've been wronged, let alone who to turn to. We're pretty well covered in the UK, and under the Trade Descriptions Act of 1968 it is a criminal offence for a trader to make false statements about goods offered for sale so if that genuine Rolex turns out to be water soluble then you can call for the cops. Don't expect the Sweeney to come squealing round the corner just yet though. The more normal approach for is to start off by talking to the Trading Standards Departments who actually enforce the Trade Descriptions Act. You'll find them at www.tradingstandards.gov.uk, unless you live in Northern Ireland in which case you want the Trading Standards Branch of the Dept. of Economic Development (www.tssni.gov.uk). The Office of Fair Trading (www.oft.gov.uk) is also on your side and will answer individual enquiries about traders you suspect of breaking the law; email them at enquiries@oft.gov.uk. If you feel that the problem lies in a misleading advert then you can also complain about it to the Advertising Standards Authority (www.asa.org.uk) who can be emailed at inquiries@asa.org.uk. Just one thing though, if a retailer has broken the law then the authorities can step in, but if it's not clear they won't get involved in individual disputes and you might have to bring your own action against a trader. If in doubt have a word with the Citizens Advice Bureau which has a Web site at www.adviceguide.org.uk, or look at the DTI's Consumer Gateway Web site at www.consumer.gov.uk.

If you do decide that you've got a genuine grievance, and that the site broke the law in ripping you off, then you have the right to take them to the small claims court. Court charges are cheaper than you think, and are set on a fixed scale so you know in advance what it's likely to cost you. In England and Wales claims up to £200 have a fixed cost of just £27. At the other end of the scale claims of up to £5000 (not my idea of a 'small' claim) carry a maximum fee of £115. There's more information available on the court system in the UK at www.courtservice.gov.uk.

Any complaint you make, let alone any action you have to bring, will be made much easier if you have a precise record of all correspondence including copies of the adverts and descriptions of goods.

Also remember that you the above bodies are all in the UK – if you're buying from a site whose only registered address is a tax haven in the Caribbean then you can reasonably expect things to get very messy if you try to take them to court. That said it doesn't mean that you're on your own just because you bought from a foreign site. The vast majority of shopping sites are in the US, and the fact that you're not an American has no bearing on the US body that investigates fraud. If a US site rips you off then you should immediately report the fact to the Federal Trade Commission who have a reputation for being extremely efficient in sorting out the bad guys. The FTC can be contacted at www.ftc.gov where you'll find a complaint form ready and waiting for just such an eventuality.

Right then, you know your rights, you know how to minimise the risks, and you know who you're gonna call if it all goes fruit shaped. Now it's time to shop.

Index